General Knowledge 2023

Published by

Diamond Power Learning

An imprint of

Diamond Pocket Books Pvt. Ltd.

X-30, Okhla Industrial Area, Phase–2, New Delhi-20

Tel : 91-011-40712200

e-mail : sales@dpb.in

website : www.diamondbook.in

Contents

1. Latest GK	2-13
2. Union Budget 2022-23 Forest survey report 2021	14-16
3. India and World History	17-35
4. India and World Geography	36-48
5. Indian Polity	49-57
6. Indian Economy	58-66
7. General Science	67-85
8. Computer	86-87
9. Miscellaneous	88-96

DIAMOND POWER LEARNING

Latest
General Knowledge

❍	**President**	Draupadi Murmu (15th)
❍	**Vice–president**	Jagdeep Dhankhar, (14th)
❍	**Prime Minister**	Mr. Narendra Modi (15th)

CENTRAL MINISTRY, 2022

Prime Minister–Narendra Modi– Prime Minister and also in-charge of: Personnel, Public Grievances and Pensions; Department of Atomic Energy; Department of Space; and All important policy issues; and All other portfolios not allocated to any Minister.

CABINET MINISTER

Ministers	Ministry

- Amit Shah –**Home and Cooperation**
- Raj Nath Singh –**Defence**
- Nirmala Sitharaman –**Finance and Corporate Affairs**
- Nitin Jairam Gadkari – **Road Transport and Highways**
- Narendra Singh Tomar– **Agriculture and Farmers Welfare**
- Dr. Subrahmanyam Jaishankar –**External Affairs**
- Arjun Munda –**Tribal Affairs**
- Smriti Zubin Irani –**Women and Child Development, Minority Affairs (add. charge)**
- Piyush Goyal–**Commerce and Industry; Consumer Affairs, Food and Public Distribution; and Textiles**
- Dharmendra Pradhan– **Education; and Skill Development and Entrepreneurship**
- Pralhad Joshi – **Parliamentary Affairs; Coal; and Mines**
- Narayan Tatu Rane– **Micro, Small and Medium Enterprises**
- Sarbananda Sonowal – **Ports, Shipping and Waterways; and AYUSH**
- Dr. Virendra Kumar– **Social Justice and Empowerment**
- Giriraj Singh –**Rural Development; and Panchayati Raj**
- Jyotiraditya M. Scindia –**Civil Aviation& Steel**
- Ashwini Vaishnaw –**Railways; Communications; and Electronics and Information Technology**
- Pashu Pati Kumar Paras –**Food Processing Industries**
- Gajendra Singh Shekhawat –**Jal Shakti**
- Kiren Rijiju –**Law and Justice**
- Raj Kumar Singh –**Power; and New and Renewable Energy**
- Hardeep Singh Puri– **Petroleum and Natural Gas; and Housing and Urban Affairs**
- Mansukh Mandaviya–**Health and Family Welfare; and Chemicals and Fertilizers**
- Bhupender Yadav– **Environment, Forest and Climate Change; and Labour and Employment**
- Dr. Mahendra Nath Pandey– **Heavy Industries**
- Parshottam Rupala`– **Fisheries, Animal Husbandry and Dairying**
- G. Kishan Reddy –**Culture,; Tourism; and Development of North Eastern Region**
- Anurag Singh Thakur **Information and Broadcasting; and Youth Affairs and Sports**

Minister of State (Independent Charge)

Ministers	Ministry

- Rao Inderjit Singh– **Statistics and Programme Implementation; Planning; and Corporate Affairs**
- Dr. Jitendra Singh– **Science and Technology; Earth Sciences; Prime Minister's Office; Personnel, Public Grievances and Pensions; Atomic Energy; and Space**

Minister of State

Ministers	Ministry

- Shripad Yesso Naik– **Ports, Shipping and Waterways; and Tourism**
- Faggansingh Kulaste– **Steel; and Rural Development**
- Prahalad Singh Patel– **Jal Shakti; and Food Processing Industries**
- Ashwini Kumar Choubey– **Consumer Affairs, Food and Public Distribution; and Environment, Forest and Climate Change**
- Arjun Ram Meghwal– **Parliamentary Affairs; and Culture**
- General (Retd.) V. K. Singh– **Road Transport and Highways; and Civil Aviation**
- Krishan Pal– **Power; and Heavy Industries**
- Danve Raosaheb Dadarao– **Railways; Coal; and Mines**
- Ramdas Athawale– **Social Justice and Empowerment**
- Sadhvi Niranjan Jyoti– **Consumer Affairs, Food and Public Distrib**ution; and Rural Development
- Dr. Sanjeev Kumar Balyan– **Fisheries, Animal Husbandry and Dairying**
- Nityanand Rai– **Home Affairs**
- Pankaj Chaowdhary– **Finance**
- Anupriya Singh Patel– **Commerce and Industry**
- Prof. S. P. Singh Baghel– **Law and Justice**
- Rajeev Chandrasekhar–**Skill Development and Entrepreneurship; and Electronics and Information Technology**
- Shobha Karandlaje– **Agriculture and Farmers Welfare**
- Bhanu Pratap Singh Verma– **Micro, Small and Medium Enterprises**
- Darshana Vikram Jardosh– T**extiles; and Railways**
- V. Muraleedharan– **External Affairs; and Parliamentary Affairs**
- Meenakashi Lekhi– **External Affairs; and Culture**
- Som Parkash– **Commerce and Industry**
- Renuka Singh Saruta– **Tribal Affairs**
- Rameswar Teli – **Petroleum and Natural Gas; and Labour and Employment**
- Kailash Choudhary– **Agriculture and Farmers Welfare**
- Annpurna Devi– **Education**
- A. Narayanaswamy– **Social Justice and Empowerment**
- Kaushal Kishore– **Housing and Urban Affairs**
- Ajay Bhatt– **Defence; and Tourism**
- B. L. Verma – **Development of North Eastern Region; and Cooperation**
- Ajay Kumar– **Home Affairs**
- Devusinh Chauhan– **Communications**
- Bhagwanth Khuba–**New and Renewable Energy; and Chemicals and Fertilizers**
- Kapil Moreshwar Patil– **Panchayati Raj**
- Pratima Bhoumik– **Social Justice and Empowerment**
- Dr. Subhas Sarkar– **Education**
- Dr. Bhagwat Kishanrao Karad– **Finance**
- Dr. Rajkumar Ranjan Singh–**External Affairs; and Education**
- Dr. Bharati Pravin Pawar–**Health and Family Welfare**
- Bishweswar Tudu–**Tribal Affairs; and of State in the Ministry of Jal Shakti**
- Shantanu Thakur–**Ports, Shipping and Waterways**
- Dr. Munjapara Mahendrabhai–**Women and Child Development; and AYUSH**
- John Barla– **Minority Affairs**
- Dr. L. Murugan– **Fisheries, Animal Husbandry and Dairying; and Information and Broadcasting**
- Nisith Pramanik– **Home Affairs; and Youth Affairs and Sports**

DIGNITARIES OF INDIA

- Chief Justice of India – **Justice D.Y. Chandrachud**
- Loksabha Speaker – **Om Birla**
- Chief CBI – **Subodh Kumar Jaiswal**
- Cabinet Secretary – **Rajiv Gauba**
- Controller and Auditor General – **Girish Chandra Murmu**
- Solicitor General - **Tushar Mehta**
- Attorney General - **R Venkataramani**
- Chief Election Commissioner – **Rajeev Kumar**
- Chairman, UPSC – **Manoj Soni**

- Chairman, National Commission for Minorities
- – **Iqbal Singh Lalpura**
- Governor, RBI – **Shakti Kanta Das**
- Chairman, UGC – **Prof. M. Jagdish Kumar**
- Chairman, Railway Board – **Vinay Kumar Tripathi**
- Director, Intelligence Bureau – **Tapan Kumar Deka**
- Chairman, FICCI – **Sanjeev Mehta**
- Chairman, ISRO – **S. Somnath**
- Chairman, Central Direct Tax Board – **Nitin Gupta**
- Chairman, 15th Finance Commission – **N.K. Singh**
- Raw Chief – **Samant Kumar Goel**
- Chairman, Air India– **Mr N Chandrasekaran**
- Deputy Chairman, Rajya Sabha – **Harivansh Narayan**

HEADS OF NATIONAL BANKS

Bank	Managing Director
State Bank of India	– **Dinesh Kumar Khara (Chairman)**
PNB	– **Atul Kumar Goel**
Bank of Baroda	– **Sanjiv Chadha**
Canara Bank	– **Lingam Venkat Prabhakar**
Union Bank of India	– **G. Rajkiran Rai**
Bank of India	– **Atanu Kumar Das**
Indian Bank	– **Shri Shanti Lal Jain**
Central Bank of India	– **Matam Venkata Rao**
Indian Overseas Bank	– **Partha Pratim Sengupta**
UCO Bank	– **Shri Soma Sankara Prasad**
Bank of Maharashtra	– **A. S. Rajeev**
Punjab & Sindh Bank	– **S Krishnan**

HEADS OF PRIVATE BANKS

Bank	M. D./C.E.O.
Axis Bank	– **Amitabh Chaudhry**
Bandhan Bank	– **Chandra S. Ghosh**
Catholic Syrian Bank	– **C. VR. Rajendran**
City Union Bank	– **Dr. N. Kamakodi**
Dhanalakshmi Bank	– **J K Shivan**
Federal Bank	– **Shyam Srinivasan**
HDFC Bank	– **Sashidhar Jagdishan**
ICICI Bank	– **Sandeep Bakshi**
IDFC Bank	– **V. Vaidyanathan**
IndusInd Bank	– **Sumant Kathpalia**
Jammu & Kashmir Bank	– **Baldev Prakash**
Karnataka Bank	– **Mahabaleshwara M. S.**
Karur Vysya Bank	– **P. R. Seshadri**
Kotak Mahindra Bank	– **Uday Kotak**
Lakshmi Vilas Bank	– **Subramanian Sundar**
Nainital Bank	– **Dinesh Pant**
RBL Bank	– **R. Subramaniakumar**
South Indian Bank	– **Murali Ramakrishnan**

DIRECTORS OF MAHARATNA COMPANIES

Company	Chairman
Bharat Heavy Electricals Ltd. (BHEL)	– **Nalin Singhal**
Coal India Ltd. (CIL)	– **Pramod Agrawal**
Gas Authority of India Ltd. (GAIL)	– **M.V. Ayyar**
Indian Oil Corporation Ltd. (IOCL)	– **Srikant Madhav Vaidhya**
Oil and Natural Gas Corporation Ltd. (ONGC)	– **Rajesh Kumar Srivastav**
Steel Authority of India Ltd. (SAIL)	– **Soma Mandal**
National Thermal Power Corporation Ltd.(NTPC)	– **Gurdeep Singh**
Bharat Petroleum Corporation Limited (BPCL)	– **Arun Kumar Singh**

GOVERNORS AND CHIEF MINISTERS

States	Chief Minister	Governer
Andhra Pradesh	Y.S. Jagan Mohan Reddy	Biswabhushan Harichandan
Arunachal Pradesh	Pema Khandu	Brigadier B.D Mishra (retd)
Assam	Himanta Biswa Sarma	Jagdish Mukhi
Bihar	Nitish Kumar	Phagu Chauhan
Chhattisgarh	Bhupesh Bhagel	Anusuiya Uikey
Goa	Pramod Sawant	PS Sreedharan Pillai
Gujarat	Bhupendra bhai Rajnikant Patel	Acharaya Devvrat
Haryana	Manohar Lal Khattar	Bandaru Dattatreya
Himachal Pradesh	Jai Ram Thakur	Rajendra Vishwanath Arlekar
Jharkhand	Hemant Soren	Ramesh Bais
Karnataka	Sri Basavaraj Bommai	Thawar Chand Gehlot
Kerala	Pinarayi Vijayan	Arif Mohammed Khan
Madhya Pradesh	Shivraj Singh Chouhan	Mangubhai Chaganbhai Patel
Maharastra	Eknath Shinde	Bhagat Singh Koshyari
Manipur	N. Biren Singh	Shri La. Ganesan
Meghalaya	Conrad Kongkal Sangma	B D Mishra (Additional Charge)
Mizoram	Zoramthanga	Dr. Kambhampati Haribabu
Nagaland	Neiphiu Rio	Jagdish Mukhi (Additional Charge)
Odisha	Naveen Patnaik	Prof. Ganesh Lal Mathur
Punjab	Bhagwant Mann Singh	Banwarilal Purohit
Rajasthan	Ashok Gehlot	Kalraj Mishra
Sikkim	Prem Singh Tamang	Ganga Prasad
Tamil Nadu	M.K Stalin	R.N. Ravi
Telangana	K.Chandrashekhar Rao	Dr. Tamilisai Soundararajan
Tripura	Manik Saha	Satyadev Narayan Arya
Uttar Pradesh	Yogi Adityanath	Anandiben Patel
Uttarakhand	Shri Pushkar Singh Dhami	Gurmit Singh
West Bengal	Mamata Banerjee	Shri La. Ganesan (Addi.charge)

Union Territories and their Administrators

- Andaman and Nicobar Islands – **Devendra Kumar Joshi**
- Chandigarh – **Shri Banwarilal Purohit ((Admn.)**
- Dadra and Nagar Haveli & Daman and Diu – **Prafulla Khoda Patel (Admn.)**
- Delhi – **Shri Vinai Kumar Saxena(LG)**
- Puducherry – **Dr. Tamilisai Soundararajan(LG)**
- Lakshadweep – **Prafulla Khoda Patel (Admn.)**
- Jammu & Kashmir – **Shri Manoj Sinha (LG)**
- Ladakh – **Radha Krishna Mathur (LG)**

HEADS OF VARIOUS MILITARY/POLICE DEPARTMENTS OF INDIA

Military/Police Department	Head	Time–Period
C.D.S. Chief	**Ret. Gen. Anil Chauhan**	**Sep., 2022 – Present**
Air Force	**Vivek Ram Choudhary**	**Sep., 2021 – Present**
Navy	**Admiral R. Hari Kumar**	**Nov., 2021 – Present**
Military	**General Manoj Pandey**	**May., 2022 – Present**
Border Security Force (BSF)	**Pankaj Kumar Singh**	**Sep., 2021 – Present**
ITBP	**Anish Dayal Singh**	**Oct., 2022 – Present**
CRPF	**Dr.Sujoy Lal Thaosen**	**Aug., 2022 – Present**
CISF	**Sheel Vardhan Singh**	**Nov, 2021 – Present**
Assam Rifles	**Pradeep Chandra Nair**	**May, 2022 – Present**
SSB	**Anish Dayal Singh (Add. Charge)**	**Oct., 2022 – Present**
National Security Guard (NSG)	**M.A. Ganapati**	**March., 2021 – Present**

HEADS OF INTERNATIONAL INSTITUTES/ORGANIZATIONS

Head	Organization	Head	Organization
Antonio Guterres (Portuguese)	• **Secretary General, United Nations Organization (UNO)**	Gerd Müller (Germany)	• **Director General, United Nations Industrial Development Organization (UNIDO)**
Abdulla Shahid (Maldives)	• **Chairman, United Nations General Assembly (UNGA)**	Catherine Russell (USA)	• **Executive Director, United Nations Child Emergency Fund (UNICEF)**
Rafael Mariano Grossi (Argentina)	• **Director General, International Atomic Energy Agency (IAEA)**	Joan E. Donoghue (USA)	• **Chairman, International Court (ICJ)**
Gilbert F. Houngbo (Togo)	• **Director General, International Labor Organization (ILO)**	Achim Steiner (Germany)	• **Administrator, United Nations Development Program (UNDP)**
Qu Dongyu (China)	• **Food and Agriculture Organizations (FAO)**	Filippo Grandi (Italy)	• **United Nations High Commissioner for Refugees (UNHCR)**
Audrey Azoulay (French)	• **Director General, United Nation Educational; Scientific and Cultural Organization (UNESCO)**	Federico Villegas (Argentina)	• **President, United Nations Human Rights Council (UNHRC)**
Sebastian Coe (Britain)	• **Chairman, International Association of Athletics Federations (IAAF)**	Macky Sall (Senegal)	• **African Union (AU)**
Tedros Adhanom Ghebreyesus (Ethiopia)	• **Director General, World Health Organization (WHO)**	Dato Lim Jock Hoi (Brunei)	• **Secretary General, ASEAN**

Kristalina Georgieva (Bulgaria)	• **Managing Director, International Monetary Fund (IMF)**	Haitham Al Ghais (Kuwait)	• **Secretary General, OPEC**
David MalpasS (USA)	• **Chairman, World Bank (WB)**	Esala Ruwan Weerakoon (Sri Lanka)	• **Secretary General, SAARC**
Ngozi Okonjo-Iweala((Nigeria)	• **Director General, World Trade Organization (WTO)**	Rawhi Fattouh (Palestine)	• **Chairman, Palestine Liberation Organization (PLO)**
Rebeca Grynspan (Costa Rica,)	• **Secretary–General of UNCTAD**	Hissein Brahim Taha (Chadi)	• **Secretary General, Organization of Islamic Cooperation (OIC)**

VARIOUS COMMITTEES AND THEIR FIELD OF WORK

Name of the Committee	Field of Work
Swaminathan	Population Policy
Jankiram	Security Transaction
Dantwala	Estimation of Unemployment
Rekhi	Indirect Tax
Sarkaria	Center–State Relation
Goswami	Industrial sickness
Mahalanobis	National Income
Rangarajan	Balance of Payment
Raja Chelaiya	Tax Reform
Malhotra	Broad Framework Of Insurance Sector
Khusro	Agricultural Credit System
Goiforiya	Improvement In The Customer service At Primary (Urban) Cooperative Banks
Bhurelal	—
Narsinham	Banking Reforms
Bhandari	Restructuring of RRB
Sachchar	Social, Economic and Educational condition of the Muslim Community of India.
Suresh Tendulkar	Measurement of poverty
S. Tarapor	Capital Account Convertibility on Rupees
Abid Hussain	On Small Scale Industries
Dr. Kirit S. Parikh	Pricing of Diesel, Petrol & LPG Products
V. S. Vyas	Agriculture and Allied Sector
Mahajan	Sugar Industry
Abhijit Sen	Long Food Policy
Besal	Banking Supervision
Ajit Kumar	Army Pay Scales
C. B. Bhave	Company information
Kelkar	Tax structure reform
Kumar Manglam Birla Report	Corporate Governance
G.V. Ramkrishnan	Disinvestment
J. J. Irani	Company Law Reforms
Malegam	Reforms In The Primary Market & Repositioning of UTI
Chandrashekhar	Venture Capital
Deepak parikh	Unit Trust of India
Justice Verma	Amendments to Criminal Law

PRESIDENTS OF INDIA

Dr. Rajendra Prasad	**1950–62**
Dr. S. Radhakrishnan	**1962–67**
Dr. Zakir Hussain	**1967–69**
V. V. Giri	**1969–69**
Justice Mohammad Hidayatullah	**1969–69**
V. V. Giri	**1969–74**
Fakhruddin Ali Ahmed	**1974–77**

B. D. Jatti	1977–77
Neelam Sanjeev Reddy	1977–82
Gyani jail Singh	1982–87
R. Venkatraman	1987–92
Dr. Shankar Dayal Sharma	1992–97
K. R. Narayanan	1997–2002
Dr. A. P. J. Abdul Kalam	2002–07
Pratibha Devi Singh Patil	2007–12
Pranab Mukherjee	2012– 2017
Ramnath Kovind	2017–2022
Draupadi Murmu 2022 -	Present

PRIME MINISTERS OF INDIA

Jawahar Lal Nehru	1947–64
Gulzari Lal Nanda	1964–64
Lal Bahadur Shashtri	1964–66
Gulzari Lal Nanda	1966–66
Indira Gandhi	1966–77
Morarji Desai	1977–79
Choudhari Charan Singh	1979–80
Indira Gandhi	1980–84
Rajiv Gandhi	1984–89
V. P. Singh	1989–90
Chandrashekhar	1990–91
P. V. Narsimha Rao	1991–96
Atal Bihari Vajpayee	1996–96
H. D. Devagowda	1996–97
I K. Gujral	1997–98
Atal Bihari Vajpayee	1998–2004
Dr. Manmohan Singh	2004–09
Dr. Manmohan Singh	2009–14
Narendra Modi	2014– Present

VICE–PRESIDENTS OF INDIA

Dr. Sarvpalli Radhkrishnan	1952–1962
Dr. Zakir Hussein	1962–1967
V. V. Giri	1967–1969
Gopal Swroop Pathak	1969–1974
B. D. Jatti	1974–1979
Justice Hidayatullah	1979–1984
R. Venkatraman	1984–1987
Dr. Shankar Dayal Sharma	1987–1992
K. R. Narayanan	1992–1997
Krishna Kant	1997–2002
Bhairo Singh Shekhawat	2002–2007
Dr. Hamid Ansari	2007–2017
M. Venkaiya Naidu Jagdeep Dhankhar	2017–2022 2022- Present

HIGH COURTS OF INDIA

S. No.	Name of the Court	Estd. Year
1.	Kolkata (Calcutta)	1862
2.	Mumbai (Bombay)	1862
3.	Chennai (Madras)	1862
4.	Allahabad	1866
5.	Karnataka	1884
6.	Patna	1916
7.	Madhya Pradesh	1956
8.	Jammu and Kashmir	1943
9.	Punjab and Haryana	1919
10.	Guwahati	1948
11.	Odisha	1948
12.	Rajasthan	1949
13.	Andhra Pradesh*	2019
14.	Kerala	1956
15.	Gujrat	1960
16.	Delhi	1966
17.	Himachal Pradesh	1971
18.	Sikkim	1975
19.	Chhatisgadh	2000
20.	Uttrakhand	2000
21.	Jharkhand	2000
22.	Manipur	2013
23.	Meghalaya	2013
24.	Tripura	2013
25.	Telangana#	1954

* (After established of high court of Telangana.)
# (Formaly known as high court of Andhra Pradesh.)

DISTRIBUTION OF SEATS IN LOK SABHA

State	Seats	State	Seats
Andhra Pradesh	25	Rajasthan	25
Arunachal Pradesh	2	Sikkim	1
Assam	14	Tamil Nadu	39
Uttrakhand	5	Karnataka	28
Bihar	40	Kerala	20
Goa	2	Uttar Pradesh	80
Gujarat	26	West Bengal	42
Chhatisgadh	11	Madhya Pradesh	29
Jharkhand	14	Telangana	17
Haryana	10	**Union Territories**	
Himachal Pradesh	4	Delhi	7
Maharashtra	48	Jammu and Kashmir	5
Manipur	2	Andaman and Nicobar Islands	1
Meghalaya	2	Chandigarh	1

Mizoram	1	Dadar and Nagar Haveli & Daman and Diu	2
Nagaland	1		
Odisha	21	Lakshdweep	1
Punjab	13	Puducherry	1
Tripura	2	Nominated Anglo Indians	2
		Ladakh	1
		Total = 545	

ALLOTMENT OF SEATS IN RAJYA SABHA (FOURTH SCHEDULE)

State	No. of Members	State	No. of Members
Andhra Pradesh	11	Rajasthan	10
Assam	7	Uttar Pradesh	31
Bihar	16	West Bengal	16
Jharkhand	6	Uttrakhand	3
Goa	1	Jammu and Kashmir	4
Gujrat	11	Nagaland	1
Haryana	5	Himachal Pradesh	3
Kerala	9	Manipur	1
Madhya Pradesh	11	Tripura	1
Chhatisgadh	5	Meghalaya	1
Tamil Nadu	18	Sikkim	1
Maharashtra	19	Mizoram	1
Karnataka	12	Arunachal Pradesh	1
Odisha	10	Delhi	3
Punjab	7	Puducherry	1
Nominated Members	12	Telangana	7
		Total = 245	

LOK SABHA SPEAKERS

G. V. Mavalankar	1952–1956
M. A. Ayangar	1956–1962
Hukum Singh	1962–1967
Neelam Sanjeev Reddy	1967–1969
Gurdayal Singh Dhillon	1969–1975
Bali Ram Bhagat	1976–1977
Neelam Sanjeev Reddy	1977–1977
K. S. Hegde	1977–1980
Balram Jakhar	1980–1989
Ravi Rai	1989–1991
Shivraj V. Patil	1991–1996
P. A. Sangma	1996–1998
G. M. C. Balyogi	1998–2002
Manohar Joshi	2002–2004
Somnath Banerjee	2004–2009
Mira Kumar	2009–2014
Sumitra Mahajan	2014–2019
Om Birla	June 2019 – Present

GOVERNORS OF RESERVE BANK OF INDIA

Osbon Smith	1935–1937
James Braid Taylor	1937–1943
C. D. Deshmukh	1943–1949
Benegal Rama Rao	1949–1957
K. G. Ambegaonkar	1957–1957
H. V. R. Ayangar	1957–1962
P. C. Bhhatacharya	1962–1967
L. K. Jha	1967–1970
B N. Adarkar	1970–1970
S Jaganathan	1970–1975
N C. Sen Gupta	1975–1975
K R. Puri	1975–1977
M Narsimhan	1977–1977
Dr. I. G. Patel	1977–1982
Dr. Manmohan Singh	1982–1985
A Ghosh	1985–1985
R N. Malhotra	1985–1990
S Venkatraman	1990–1992
Dr. C. Rangrajan	1992–1997
Dr. Bimal Jalan	1997–2003
Dr. Y. V. Reddy	2003–2008
Dr. D. Subbarao	2008–2013
Raghuram Rajan	2013–2016
Urjit Patel	2016–2018
Shakti Kant Das	2018–Present

COMPTROLLER AND AUDITOR GENERAL

V. Narhari Rao	1948–1954
A K. Chanda	1954–1960
A K. Rao	1960–1966
S Rangnathan	1966–1972
A Bakshi	1972–1978
Gyan Prakash	1978–1984
T N. Chaturvedi	1984–1990
C G. Somaiya	1990–1996
V K. Shunglu	1996–2002
V N. Kaul	2002–2008
Vinod Roy	2008–2013
Shashikant Sharma	2013–2017
Rajiv Mehrishi	2017 – 2021
Girish Chandra Murmu	2021- Present

ATTORNEY GENERALS OF INDIA

M. C. Sitalwad	1950–1963
C K. Daftari	1963–1968
Niran Dey	1968–1977
S V. Gupta	1977–1979
L N. Sinha	1979–1983
K Parasaran	1983–1989
Soli J. Sorabji	1989–1990
G Ramaswami	1990–1992
Milan K. Banerjee	1992–1996
Ashok K. Desai	1996–1998
Soli J. Sorabji	1998–2004
Milan K. Banerjee	2004–2009
Ghulam E. Vahanvati	2009–2014
Mukul Rohtagi	2014–2017
K.K. Venugopal	2017 – 2022
R Venkataramani	Sep.2022- Present

IMPORTANT DAYS OF INDIA

26th January	Republic Day
30th January	Sorrow Day
28th February	National Science Day
3rd March	National Defense Day
4th March	National Security Day
11th May	National Technology Day
26th July	Kargil Victory Day
9th August	Quit India Day
15th August	Independence Day
20th August	Communal Harmony Day
29th August	National Sports Day
5th September	Teacher's Day
2nd October	Gandhi Birth Anniversary
8th October	Indian Air Force Day
10th October	National Postal Day
14th November	Children's Day
4th December	Navy Day
7th December	Armed Forces Flag Day
18th December	Minority Rights Day
23rd December	Farmer's Day

IMPORTANT DAYS OF THE WORLD

26th January	International Custom day	5th June	World Environment Day
4th February	World Cancer Day	12th June	World Child Labor Prevention Day
20th February	World Social Justice Day	21st June	World Yoga Day
8th March	International Woman's Day	11th July	World Population Day
15th March	World Consumer Rights Day	6th August	Hiroshima Day
21st March	World Forestry Day	9th August	Nagasaki Day
22nd March	World Water day	12th August	International Youth Day
23rd March	World Weather Science Day	19th August	World Photography Day
24th March	World T.B Day	8th September	World Literacy day
7th April	World Health Day	16th September	World Ozone Day
18th April	World Heritage Day	21st September	World Peace Day
22nd April	Earth Day	27th September	World Tourist Day
23rd April	World Book and Copyright Day	1st October	International Day of Older Persons
1st May	International Labor Day	4th October	World Animal Welfare Day
3rd May	Freedom of Press Day	9th October	World Post Day
8th May	World Red Cross Day	16th October	World Food Day
12th May	International Nurse Day	24th October	United Nations Day
15th May	International Family Day	14th November	Diabetes Day

17th May	World Telecommunication Day	1st December	World AIDS Day
24th May	Commonwealth Day	10th December	Human Rights Day
31st May	Tobacco Prevention Day		

FIRST WOMAN IN INDIA

First woman prime minister	**Indira Gandhi**
First woman Governor in independent India	**Sarojini Naidu**
First woman ambassador	**C B. Muthamma**
First woman judge in the Supreme Court	**Fatima Bibi**
First woman to climb mount Everest	**Bachhendri Pal**
First woman to climb mount Everest twice	**Santosh Yadav**
First woman pilot in the Indian Air Force	**Harita Kaur Dayal**
First graduate woman	**Kadambini Ganguly and Chandramukhi Basu (1883)**
First woman airline pilot	**Durba Banerjee**
First woman to win a gold medal in the Asian Games	**Kamlijit Sandhu**
First woman chairman of United Nations General Assembly	**Vijaya Lakshmi Pandit**
First woman chairman of UPSC	**Rose Million Bethyu**
First woman Police Director General	**Kanchan Choudhary Bhattacharya**
The first and last woman Muslim ruler of India	**Razia Sultan**
First woman to receive the Ashok Chakra	**Neerja Bhanot**
First woman awarded with Gyanpith award	**Ashapurna Devi**
First Nobel laureate woman	**Mother Theresa**
First woman to be awarded with Bharat Ratna	**Indira Gandhi**
First woman chief minister of an Indian state	**Sucheta Kriplani**
First Chief Justice of High Court	**Lila Seth (Himachal Pradesh High Court)**
First Miss World	**Rita Faria**
First woman lawyer	**Cornelia Sorabji**
First woman to be awarded with Lenin Peace Prize	**Aruna Asaf Ali**
First woman to win a medal at Olympic games	**Karnam Malleshvari**
The woman with a world record in Power Lifting	**Sumita Laha (1989)**
First woman astronaut	**Kalpana Chawla**

AREA, POPULATION AND DECADAL POPULATION GROWTH RATE OF INDIA AND ITS STATES/UNION TERRITORIES

S. No.	India/State/ Union Territory	Area Sq. KM	Total Population (2011)			Decadal Growth Rate (2001–11)
			Person	Men	Women	

	India	3287469	1210269573	623121843	587447730	17.7
1.	Jammu and Kashmir	222236	12541302	6640662	5900640	23.6
2.	Himachal Pradesh	55673	6864602	3481873	3382729	12.9
3.	Punjab	50362	27743338	14639365	13103873	13.9
4.	Chandigarh	114	1055450	580663	474787	17.2
5.	Uttrakhand	53483	10086292	5137773	4948519	18.8
6.	Haryana	44212	25351462	13491734	11856728	19.9
7.	Delhi, N. C. R.	1483	16787941	8987326	7800615	21.2
8.	Rajasthan	342239	68548437	35550997	32997440	21.3
9.	Uttar Pradesh	240928	199812341	104480510	95331831	20.2
10.	Bihar	94163	104099452	54278157	49821295	25.4
11.	Sikkim	7096	610577	323070	287507	12.9
12.	Arunachal Pradesh	83743	1383727	713912	669815	26.0
13.	Nagaland	16579	1978502	1024649	953853	–0.6
14.	Manipur	22327	2570390	1290171	1280219	18.6
15.	Mizoram	21081	1097206	555339	541867	23.18
16.	Tripura	10486	3673917	1874376	1799541	14.5
17.	Meghalaya	22429	2966889	1491832	1475057	27.9
18.	Assam	78438	3120576	15939443	15266133	17.1
19.	West Bengal	88752	91276115	46809027	44467088	13.8
20.	Jharkhand	79716	32988134	16930315	16057819	22.4
21.	Odisha	155707	41974218	21212136	20762082	14.0
22.	Chhatisgadh	135192	25545198	12832895	12712303	22.6
23.	Madhya Pradesh	308252	72626809	37612306	35014503	20.3
24.	Gujrat	196244	60439692	31491260	28948432	19.3
25.	Daman and Diu	111	243227	150301	92946	53.8
26.	Dadra and Nagar Haveli	491	343709	193760	149949	55.9
27.	Maharashtra	307713	112374333	58243056	54131277	16.0
*28.	Andhra Pradesh	275045	84580777	42442146	42138631	11.0
29.	Karnataka	191791	61095297	30966657	30128640	15.6
30.	Goa	3702	1458545	739140	719405	8.2
31.	Lakshdweep	30	64473	33123	31350	6.3
32.	Kerala	38852	33406061	16027412	17378649	4.9
33.	Tamil Nadu	130060	72147030	36137975	36009055	15.6
34.	Puducherry	490	1247953	612511	635442	28.1

35.	Andaman and Nicobar Islands	8249	380581	202871	177710	6.9

POPULATION DENSITY AND SEX RATIO IN INDIA AND ITS STATES/UNION TERRITORIES

S. No.	India/State/ Union Territory	Population Density 2011	Sex Ratio 2011	Infant Population 2011 (0–6 years)	Ratio of Infant in Total Population 2011	Infant Sex Ratio 2011
	India	**382**	**943**	**164478150**	**13.6**	**919**
1.	**Jammu and Kashmir**	**124**	889	2018905	16.1	862
2.	**Himachal Pradesh**	**123**	972	777898	11.3	909
3.	**Punjab**	**551**	895	3076219	11.1	846
4.	**Chandigarh**	**9258**	818	119434	11.3	880
5.	**Uttrakhand**	**189**	963	1355814	13.4	890
6.	**Haryana**	**573**	879	3380721	13.3	834
7.	**Delhi, N. C. R.**	**11320**	868	2012454	12.0	871
8.	**Rajasthan**	**200**	928	10649504	15.5	888
9.	**Uttar Pradesh**	**829**	912	30791331	15.4	902
10.	**Bihar**	**1106**	918	19133964	18.4	935
11.	**Sikkim**	**86**	890	64111	10.6	957
12.	**Arunachal Pradesh**	**17**	938	212138	15.3	972
13.	**Nagaland**	**119**	931	291071	14.7	943
14.	**Manipur**	**115**	992	338254	13.2	936
15.	**Mizoram**	**52**	976	168531	15.4	970
16.	**Tripura**	**350**	960	458014	12.5	957
17.	**Meghalaya**	**132**	989	568536	19.2	970
18.	**Assam**	**398**	958	4638130	14.9	962
19.	**West Bengal**	**1028**	950	10581466	11.6	956
20.	**Jharkhand**	**414**	949	5389495	16.3	948
21.	**Odisha**	**270**	979	5273194	12.6	941
22.	**Chhatisgadh**	**189**	991	3661689	14.3	969
23.	**Madhya Pradesh**	**276**	931	10809395	14.9	918
24.	**Gujrat**	**308**	919	7777262	12.9	890
25.	**Daman and Diu**	**2191**	618	26934	11.1	904
26.	**Dadra and Nagar Haveli**	**700**	774	50895	14.8	926

27.	**Maharashtra**	**365**	929	13326517	11.9	894
*28.	**Andhra Pradesh**	**308**	993	9142802	10.8	939
29.	**Karnataka**	**319**	973	7161033	11.7	948
30.	**Goa**	**394**	973	144611	9.9	942
31.	**Lakshdweep**	**2149**	947	7255	11.3	911
32.	**Kerala**	**860**	1084	3472955	10.4	964
33.	**Tamil Nadu**	**555**	996	7423832	10.3	943
34.	**Puducherry**	**2547**	1037	132858	10.6	967
35.	**Andaman and Nicobar Islands**	**46**	876	40878	10.7	968

* Since Telangana was carved out from Andhra Pradesh June 2014, so all of the census 2011 Data of Telangana are given with Andhra Pradesh.

Union Budget 2022-23

- Finance Minister Nirmala Sitharaman on February 1,2022 presented the Union Budget 2022-23. The government has projected growth at 8% to 8.5% compared with an estimated 9.2% for the current fiscal year and a 6.6% contraction the previous year.

Budget Highlights

- **Expenditure :** The government proposes to spend Rs 39,44,909 crore in 2022-23, which is an increase of 4.6% over the revised estimate of 2021-22. In 2021-22, total expenditure is estimated to be 8.2% higher than budget estimate.
- **Receipts** : The receipts (other than borrowings) in 2022-23 are expected to be to Rs 22,83,713 crore, an increase of 4.8% over revised estimate of 2021-22. In 2021-22, total receipts (other than borrowings) are estimated to be 10.2% higher than the budget estimates.
- **GDP :** The government has estimated a nominal GDP growth rate of 11.1% in 2022-23 (i.e., real growth plus inflation).
- **Deficits :** Revenue deficit in 2022-23 is targeted at 3.8% of GDP, which is lower than the revised estimate of 4.7% in 2021-22. Fiscal deficit in 2022-23 is targeted at 6.4% of GDP, lower than the revised estimate of 6.9% of GDP in 2021-22 (marginally higher than the budget estimate of 6.8% of GDP). Interest expenditure at Rs 9,40,651 crore is estimated to be 43% of revenue receipts.
- **Ministry allocations** : Among the top 13 ministries with the highest allocations, in 2022-23, the highest percentage increase in allocation is observed in the Ministry of Communications (93%), followed by the Ministry of Road Transport and Highways (52%), and the Ministry of Jal Shakti (25%).
- **Communications** : Allocation to the Ministry of Communications is estimated to increase by Rs 50,890 crore (93%) in 2022-23, over the revised estimate of 2021-22. This is mainly on account of capital infusion of Rs 44,720 crore in BSNL.
- **Road Transport and Highways** : Allocation to the Ministry of Road Transport and Highways is estimated to increase by Rs 67,959 crore (52%)

in 2022-23, over the revised estimate of 2021-22. This is mainly on account of an increase in investment in National Highway Authority of India (Rs 1,34,015 crore in 2022-23 as compared to Rs 65,060 crore in 2021-22).

- In 2021-22, transfer to states as support for COVID-19 vaccines was Rs 39,000 crore, higher than the budget estimate of Rs 35,000 crore. Allocation for 2022-23 is Rs 5,000 crore.

Expenditure on Subsidies

- In 2022-23, the total expenditure on subsidies is estimated to be Rs 3,55,639 crore, a decrease of 27.1% from the revised estimate of 2021-22.
- **Food subsidy :** Allocation to food subsidy is estimated at Rs 2,06,831 crore in 2022-23, a 27.8% decrease over the revised estimate of 2021-22. A higher level of food subsidy was budgeted in 2020-21 and 2021-22 mainly on account of: (i) Pradhan Mantri Garib Kalyan Ann Yojana, which provides for free foodgrains to poor to mitigate the impact of COVID-19, and (ii) clearing loans of Food Corporation of India.
- **Fertiliser subsidy:** Expenditure on fertiliser subsidy is estimated at Rs 1,05,222 crore in 2022-23. This is a decrease of Rs 34,900 crore from the revised estimate of 2021-22. Fertiliser subsidy for 2021-22 was increased substantially under the supplementary demands in December 2021. This was in response to a sharp increase in international prices of raw materials used in the manufacturing of fertilisers.
- **Petroleum subsidy** : Petroleum subsidy consists of subsidy for LPG and Kerosene. No kerosone subsidy has been budgeted for either 2021-22 or 2022-23. Expenditure on LPG subsidy is estimated to decrease by 10.8% to Rs 5,813 crore in 2022-23.
- **Other subsidies** : Expenditure on other subsidies includes interest subsidies for various government schemes, subsidies for the price support scheme for agricultural produce, and assistance to state agencies for procurement, among others. In 2022-23, the expenditure on these other subsidies is estimated to decrease by 31% over the revised estimate of 2021-22.
- Mahatma Gandhi National Rural Employment Guarantee Scheme (MGNREGS) has the highest allocation in 2022-23 at Rs 73,000 crore. This is a decrease of 25.5% over the revised estimate of 2021-22. In 2021-22, allocation to the scheme has increased by 34.2% from Rs 73,000 crore at the budget stage to Rs 98,000 crore at the revised stage, to mitigate the impact of second wave of COVID-19.
- The PM-KISAN scheme (income support to farmers) has the second highest allocation in 2022-23 at Rs 68,000 crore. Allocation to the scheme has seen a marginal increase of 0.7% over the revised estimate of 2021-22.
- Key schemes with the comparatively higher increase in allocation in 2022-23 include: (i) Pradhan Mantri Gram Sadak Yojana (35.7%), (ii) Jal Jeevan Mission (33.3%), and (iii) National Education Mission (28.4%).
- Expenditure on Scheduled Caste and Scheduled Tribe sub-plans and schemes for welfare of women, children and NER

INDIA STATE OF FOREST REPORT - 2021

- The Ministry of Environment, Forest and Climate Change recently released the State of Forest Report 2021. It is an assessment of India's forest and tree cover, published every two years by the Forest Survey of India. The first survey was published in 1987, and ISFR 2021 is the 17th.
- **Increase in Forest Cover-**
- The report says that there has been a continuous growth of forest cover in India. The current forest cover of India is 7,13,789 square kilometres. In the last two years, the forest and tree cover has increased by 1,540 square kilometres. Around 21.71% of the land area is under forest cover. In 2019, it was 21.67%.
- Tree cover in the country has increased by 721 square kilometres.
- Three categories of forests are surveyed – very dense forests (canopy density over 70%), moderately dense forests (40-70%) and open forests (10-40%). Scrubs (canopy density less than 10%) are also surveyed but not categorised as forests.
- **Top three Tiger Reserves showing increasing forest cover–**
  - Buxa (West Bengal)- 238.80 sq km
  - Anamalai (Tamil Nadu)- 120.78 sq km and Indravati (Chhattisgarh)- 64.48 sq km
- **Increase/Decrease in Forests:**
  - The states that have shown the highest increase in forest cover are Telangana (3.07%), Andhra Pradesh (2.22%) and Odisha (1.04%).
  - Five states in the Northeast – Arunachal Pradesh, Manipur, Meghalaya, Mizoram and Nagaland have all shown loss in forest cover.
- **States with Highest Forest Area/ Cover:**
  - Area-wise – Madhya Pradesh has the largest forest cover in the country followed by Arunachal Pradesh, Chhattisgarh, Odisha and Maharashtra.
  - In terms of forest cover as percentage of total geographical area, the top five States are Mizoram, Arunachal Pradesh, Meghalaya, Manipur and Nagaland.
- **Percentage-wise Forest Cover: In terms of forest cover as a percentage of total geographical area, the top five States are-**
  - Mizoram (84.53%),
  - Arunachal Pradesh (79.33%),
  - Meghalaya (76.00%),
  - Manipur (74.34%) and
  - Nagaland (73.90%).
- Mangroves– Mangroves have shown an increase of 17 sq km. India's total mangrove cover is now 4,992 sq km.
- **Top three states showing mangrove cover increase are-**
  - Odisha (8 sq km)
  - Maharashtra (4 sq km) and
  - Karnataka (3 sq km).

INDIAN AND WORLD HISTORY

The word 'history' is derived from the Greek word 'historia', it means inquiry or information gained through investigation or the study of the bygone/ past. Herodotus, a 5th-century BCE Greek historian is considered within the Western tradition to be the "father of history", and, along with his contemporary Thucydides, helped form the foundations of modern history.

Ancient Indian History (2500-1750 BC)

- Father of history – **Herodotus**
- Indus Valley Civilisation was famous for – **well planned cities**
- The main occupation of the people of Indus Valley Civilisation was – **agriculture**
- The main crops of Indus people were – **barley and wheat**
- The easternmost and westernmost sites of Indus Valley Civilisation are – **Alamgirpur (Meerut, U.P) and Sutkagen Dor (Baluchistan, Pakistan)**
- The first person to provide information about Harappan civilisation was – **Charles Masson (1826 A.D)**
- The incharge of archaeological excavation of Harappa and Mohenjo-daro – **Sir John Marshal**
- Harappan civilisation was – **bronze age civilisation**

Ancient and Modern Names of the Rivers	
Ancient Name	**Modern Name**
Vitasta	Jhelum
Askini	Chenab
Vipasa	Baes
Purushn	Ravi
Shatudri	Sutlej
Kubha	Kabul
Krumu	Kurram
Gomti	Gomal
Drishdwati	Ghaggar

- The script of Indus civilisation was – **pictorial**
- The kings of Egypt were called – **Pharaoh**
- Kharosthi script was written – **from right to left**
- Swastika symbol first appeared in – **Indus civilisations**
- The first invention made by early humans was – **fire**
- Fire was the greatest invention of – **Palaeolithic period**
- The first domesticated animal was – **dog**

Indus valley Civilisation: Facts at a Glance

Main Site	Adjacent River	Excavation Year	Excavator	Location
Harappa	Ravi	1921	Dayaram Sahni	Montgomari District (West Punjab, Pakistan)
Mohejo-daro	Sindhu	1922	Rakhal Das Banerjee	Larkana District (Sindh, Pakistan)
Sutkagan Dor	Dast	1927	Aurel stein	Baluchistan (Pakistan)
Chanhu-daro	Sindhu	1931	Gopal Majumdar	Sindh (Pakistan)
Kalibangan	Ghaggar	1954	Brrijwasi Lal and B. K. Thapar	Ganganagar District (Rajasthan)
Kot Diji	Sindhu	1953	Fazal Ahmed	Khair Pur (Sindh)
Rangpur	Bhadar	1953-54	Rangnath Rao	Kathiawar District (Gujrat)
Ropar	Sutlej	1953-56	Yagdutt Sharma	Ropar (Punjab)
Lothal	Bhogwa	1957-58	Rangnath Rao	Ahmedabad (Gujrat)
Alamgirpur	Hindon	1958	Yagdutt Sharma	Meerut (U.P)
Banawali	Rangoi	1974	Ravinder Singh Bisht	Hisar (Haryana)

Time Period of Harappan Civilization	
Scholar	**Time Period**
Sir John Marshal	3250-2750 B.C
Fair Servis	2000-1500 B.C
R. S. Sharma	2500-1800 B.C
Ernest Mackay	2800-2500 B.C
Mortimer Wheeler	2500-1500 B.C
Madhosvroop Vats	3500-2700 B.C
George F. Dales	2900-1900 B.C
C. J. Ged	2350-1700 B.C
N.C.E.R.T	2500-1800 B.C

- Indus valley civilisation was a – **Proto-historical civilisation**
- Harappa is located on the bank of – **Ravi river**
- The port town of Indus valley civilisatison was – **Lothal**
- Indus people were not aware of – **iron**
- Mohenjo-daro is located in – **Pakistan**
- Mohenjo-daro was excavated by -**Rakhal Das Banerjee**
- The bronze statue of dancing girl was found from - **Mohejo-Daro**
- The largest building found at Mohenjo Daro is – **granary**
- The most famous building found at Mohenjo Daro is a- **Grand bathroom**
- Ancient Mesopotamia (modern Iraq called – **the land between two rivers**
- Harappa was excavated under the leadership of – **Dayaram Sahni (in 1921)**
- The people of Indus valley used to worship – **Mother Goddess**
- The total number of Puranas (composed during Gupta period) is –**18**
- The oldest Purana is – **Matsyapurana**
- The composer of Puranas are –**Lomharsh and Ugrshrwa**
- The total number of Vedas and Vedangas is – **4 and 6 respectively**

Major Indian Philosophies	
Philosophy	**Founder**
Nyaya Darshan	Maharshi Gautam
Sankhya Darshan	Maharshi Kapil
Meemansa Darshan	Maharshi Jemini
Yoga Darshan	Maharshi Patanjali
Vedenta Darshan Maharshi Badrayan	Sutlej
Lingayata Darshan Maharshi Vasavraja	Kabul
Vaisheshik Darshan	Maharshi Kanaada
Gomti	Gomal
Drishdwati	Ghaggar

Major Religions, their House of Worship and Holy Books		
Religion	**House of Worship**	**Holy Book**
Judaism	Sysnagogue	Torah (Old testament)
Parsi	Fire Temple	Zend Avesta
Sikh	Gurudwara	Guru Granth Sahib
Islam	Masjid	Quran
Christianity	Church	Bible
Hinduism	Mandir	Ramayana & Mahabharata

- The total number of Upnishdas is –**108 (13 authentic)**
- The first Muslim to study Puranas was – **Al-Biruni**
- The central theme of upnishdas is – **philosophy**
- The central theme of Brahman scriptures is – **religious rituals**
- The oldest Veda is – **Rigveda (1028 Suktas)**
- The Veda composed in both prose and poetry is – **Yajurveda**
- Shatpath Brahman is related to – **Yajurveda**
- The Veda that is a collection of occult practices is – **Atharv Veda**
- The Veda that is considered as progenitor of Indian music is - **Samveda**
- Gayatri Mantra is originally from -**Rigveda**
- The composer of Gayatri Matra –**Vishwamitra**
- Gayatri Mantra is dedicated to – **Surya Deva (Sun god)**
- The term 'Gotra' is mentioned in – **Atharv Veda**
- The pioneer of Bhagwat Dharma – **Krishna**
- Bhakti movement was started by -**Alvar saints**
- The chief source of information about the Aryans -**Rigveda**
- The river mentioned highest times in Rigveda is -**Sindhu**
- The holiest river mentioned in the Rigveda is - **Sarasvati**
- The chief deity mentioned in Rigveda - **Indra (Purandar)**
- The newest Mandala added into Rigveda - **10th Mandala**
- The Mandala in Rigveda completely devoted to Soma is – **9th Mandala**
- 'Satyamev Jayate' is derived from – **Mundkopnishada**

- The composer of ancient Hindu law – **Manu**
- The oldest Smriti is – **Manusmriti**
- The writer of 'Mitakshra' – **Vigyaneshwar**
- The original name of Mahabharata – **Jai Samhita**
- The title of Persian translation of Mahabharata (written by Veda Vyasa) – **Razm Namah**
- Aryans came into India around – **1500 BC**
- The Aryans first settled in – **Punjab and Afghanistan**
- The language of Rig Vedic Aryans – **Sanskrit**
- Aryans came to India from – **Central Asia**
- The exponent of shunyvad – **Nagarjun**

Gautam Buddha and Buddhism

- Buddha was born at- **Lumbini (563 B.C)**
- Buddha died at - **Kushinagar (483 B.C)**
- The event of Buddha's death is known as - **Mahabhinishkramana**
- Buddha's first sermon is known as - **Dharma-chakra-pravartana**
- Buddha delivered his first sermon at - **Sarnath**
- Buddha delivered his sermons in - **Pali language**
- Buddha delivered maximum number of sermons at - **Sravasti**
- The Triple Gems of Buddhism is -**Buddha, Dhamma and Sangha**
- The first woman to convert to Buddhism - **Goutami, the mother of Gutam Buddha**
- First Buddhist Meeting(Sangiti) was held during the reign of - **Ajatashatru (at Rajgrih)**
- Fourth Buddhist Meeting(Sangiti) was held during the reign of - **Kanishka (in Kundalvana, Kashmir)**
- The order of venues where Buddhist Meetings were held - **Rajgrih, Vaishali, Patliputra, Kashmir**
- Stories of Buddha's previous lives are known as - **Jataka**
- Which scripture is drawn on the walls of Ajanta caves - **Jataka**
- The main scripture of Buddhism - **Pitak**
- The house of worship of Buddhists - **Chaitya Mandap (pavilion)**
- The writer of 'Budha-charit' - **Ashwaghosha**
- The pioneer of 'Ajivak' sect - **Makhli Goshala**
- The beginning of Hijri calendar –**622 A.D**
- Sikhism began around – **1500 A. D (16th century)**

Jain Meeting (Sangiti)

Meeting	Place	Head	Reigning King
First,322 B.C	Patliputra	Sthul bhadra	Chandra gupta First
Second, 512 A.D	Vallabhi, (Gujrat)	Devardhi	Kshmashrvana

- Sufism developed in – **9th century**
- Prophet Hazrat Muhammad (the pioneer of Islam) was born in – **570 A. D (in Mecca)**
- The king who built the Surya Mandir (Sun Temple) of Konark – **Narsingh Dev (13th century A. D)**
- The sun temple of Konark, often called as the -**Black Pagoda**
- The first Tirthankar of Jainism – **Rishabh Dev**

Mahavir and Jainism

- The last (24th) Tirthankara of Jainism – **Mahavir**
- The biography of Jain Tirthankara is mentioned in – **Kalpsutra**
- Mahavir was born at – **Vaishali (540 B. C)**
- Mahavir died at – **Pavapuri (468 B. C)**
- Which Varna did Mahavir belong to – **Kshatriya**
- The first follower of Mahavir was – **Jamali (son-in-law)**
- Mahavir and Buddha both preached during the reign of – **Bimbisar, the king of Magadha**
- The triple gems of Jainism – **Samyak Darshan** (right thinking), **Samyak Gyan (right knowledge), Samyak Achran (right conduct)**
- Two sects of Jainism – **Shvetambar and Digambar**
- The ultimate goal of Jainism is – **attainment of Moksha**
- First Jain Congregation (322 B. C) was organized – **in Patliputra, during the reign of Chandragupta Mourya**
- Second Jain Congregation (512 A. D) was headed by – **Devardhi Kshama-shravana**
- Jain literature is known as – Agama
- Jesus was born in – **4 B.C, in Bethlehem**
- Jesus was crucified in – **33rd A. D (on Friday, by Roman governor Pontius Pilate)**

Buddhist Congregations

Congregation	Date	Place	Head	Reigning King
1st Buddhist Congregation	483 B. C	Rajgrih	Mahakashyap	Ajatshatru
2nd Buddhist Congregation	383 B. C	Vaishali	Sabakami	Kalashok
3rd Buddhist Congregation	251 B. C	Patliputra	Moggli Putta	Ashok
4th Buddhist Congregation	1st century A.D	Kundalvan	Vasumitra/Ashwaghosh	Kalashok

India during Mauryan Period (322 – 185 B.C)

- Capital of Magadha–**Giribrij (Rajgih)**
- The list of 16 Mahajanpadas is provided in – **Anguttar Nikaaya**
- The founder of Shishunag dynasty – **Shishunag**
- The founder of Patliputra – **Udayin**
- Patliputra is situated at – **the confluence of the Ganges and Son rivers**
- The founder of Haryak dynasty – **Bimbisara**
- The king who was known as 'Amitraghat' – **Bindusara**
- The capital of 'Avanti' Janpada – **Ujjain**
- The last ruler of Nanda dynasty – **Dhananand**
- The first foreign ruler to invade India in 326 B.C – **Alexander**
- The battle between Alexander and Poras (in Punjab) is known as – **The War of Hidespese (Vitasta)**
- The death year of Alexander – **323 B.C (Babylon)**
- The founder of Mourya dynasty – **Chandra Gupta Mourya**
- The information about Mourya dynasty is recorded in – **Arth Shashtra and Vishnu Purana**
- Sudarshan Lake was constructed by – **Chandra Gupta Mourya**
- Chandra Gupta was the follower of – **Jainism**
- The mentor and Prime Minister of Chandra Gupta Mourya – **Chanakya**
- 'Arth Shashtra', the book written by Chanakya (Vishnugupta or Koutilya) is a treatise on the theme of – **Administration**
- The Jainism instructor of Chandra Gupta – **Bhadra Bahu**
- The famous Greek intellectual who attended the court of Chandra Gupta Mourya – **Megasthnese (the writer of 'Indica')**
- Chandr Gupta spent his last days (death 298 B. C) at – **Shravanbelgola (Karnataka)**
- The ruler who converted into Jainism during his last days – **Chandra Gupta Mourya**
- The ruler who started the tradition of epigraphs/inscriptions – **Ashoka**
- Ashoka converted to Buddhism after the incident of – **Kalinga war (261 B.C)**
- Ashoka sent Buddhist missionaries to Sri Lanka – **Mahendra and Sanghmitra**
- Ashoka's coronation took place in – **269 B. C**
- The longest pillar of Ashoka – **The Seventh Pilllar**
- The name 'Ashoka' appears in – **Mosky (Andhra Pradesh) and Gurjara (Madhya Pradesh) inscriptions**
- Ashoka has mentioned himself as the ruler of Magadha in – **Bhabru/Bairat pillar edict (Jaipur, Rajasthan)**
- The account of victory and destruction caused in Kalinga war is mentioned in – **13th inscription of Ashoka**
- Sanchi stupa was built by – **Ashoka**
- Srinagar was established by – **Ashoka**
- Who discovered the Ashokan inscription in 1750 A. D – **Father Tefanthler**
- The scholar who deciphered the Ashokan inscriptions for the first time – **James Princep (1837 A. D)**
- Ashoka died in the year – **232 B. C**
- Allahabad Prashasti (eulogy) inscription provides information

Vedas : Their Brahmans and Up-Vedas

Veda	Brahman	Up-Veda
Rigveda	Aitreya and Kaushitaki	Ayurveda
Yajurveda	Shatpath	Dhanurveda
Samveda	Panchvish	Gandharva Veda
Atharv Veda	Gopath	Shilpveda

Monuments of the Gupta Period

Temple	Location
Parvati Temple	Nachna Kuthar (MP)
Shiva Temple	Bhumra (Nagod, MP)
Dashavatar Temple	Devgarh (Jhansi, MP)
Varah and Vishnu Temple	Saraj (MP)
Vishnu Temple	Tigwan (Jabalpur, MP)
Lakshman Temple	Bhitargaon (Kanpur, UP)

about – **Samudra Gupta**
- The last ruler of Mouryan dynasty – **Vrihadrath**
- The founder of Shunga dynasty – **Pushyamitra Shung**
- The last ruler of Shunga dynasty – **Devbhuti**
- The first Greek ruler to enter in Indian territory – **Demitrius 1st**
- The ruler who defeated Demitrius 1st – **Pushyamitra Shunga**
- How many Ashwamedha Yagyas did **Pushyamitra Shunga organized – two**
- The founder of Satvahan dynasty – **Simuk**
- Dashraj war (the war of ten kings) was fought at – **The banks of Prushni (Ravi) river**
- The fist rulers to issue gold coins – **Indo-Greeks**
- The coins of pure gold were issued by – **The Kushanas**
- The highest number of gold coins were issued during – **The Gupta period**
- Lead coins were issued by – **Satvahan rulers**
- Silver coins were issued for the first time by – **Chandra Gupta second (Vikramaditya)**
- The founder of Kushana dynasty – **Kanishka**
- The first capital of Kanishka – **Purushpur**
- The second capital of Kanishka – **Mathura**
- Who introduced the Shaka calender – **Kanishka (78 A. D)**
- The statues were first started to be built during – **Kushana period**

Gupta Period (320 A.D to 520 A.D)

- The founder of Gupta dynasty – **Shri Gupta**
- Temples were first built during – **The Gupta period**
- The Vimana style of architecture came into vogue during – **the Chola dynasty**
- The decimal system came into use during – **the Gupta period**
- The national calendar of India is based on – **the Saka calender**
- Charaka is known as – **The Father of Ayurveda**
- Silk Route was opened by – **Kanishka**
- The last ruler of Kushana dynasty was – **Vasudeva**

Provincial Capitals in Ashok's India

Uttrapath	Takshsila
Dakshinapath	Suvarngiri
Avanti	Ujjain
Madhya Kshetra	Patliputra
Kalinga	Tosali

Sixteen Mahajanpadas

Mahajanpad	Capital
Anga	Champa
Kashi	Varanasi
Magadha	Girivraj (Rajgrih)
Avanti	Ujjayini/Mahishmati
Vatsa	Kaushambi
Gandhara	Takshshila
Kamboja	Hatak
Kuru	Indraprastha
Panchal	Kampilya
Ashmaka	Potan or Potali
Malla	Kushinara
Chedi	Shuktimati
Shurshen	Mathura
Matsya	Viratnagar
Vajji	Videh or Mithila
Kaushala	Sravasti/Ayodhya

- The information about Gupta dynasty is provided in – **Vayu Purana**
- The author who called Samudra Gupta 'the Napoleon of India' – **Vincent Arthur Smith**
- Which ruler is depicted on his coins as a Veena (lyre) player – **Samudra Gupta**
- The court poet of Samudra Gupta – **Harishen**
- Famous Chinese traveller came to India during the reign of – **Chandra Gupta II (5th century A. D)**
- Which city did Chandra Gupta II (Vikramaditya) select for his second capital – **Ujjain**
- Vikrami calendar was started in – **58 B. C**
- The names of the silver and gold currencies of the Guptas – **Rupak and Dinar respectively**
- The founder of Nalanda university – **Kumar Gupta**
- The Nalanda university destroyer by – **Bakhtiyar Khalji (commander of Muhammad Ghouri)**
- The founder of Vikramshila university – **Dharampal (the ruler belonging to Pala dynasty from 770-810 A.D)**
- Iron pillar of Raja Chandra, situated at Mehrauli, was built by – **Chandra Gupta II**
- Gangai Kond was the epithet of

Sangama Councils

First Sangama:
Head: Agastya
Location: Madura
Important books: Mudukuram, Akattiyam etc.

Second Sangama:
Head: Agastya and Tolakkapiyar
Location: Kapaadapuram
Important books: Tolakkapiyam Agattiyam, Mapuranam

Third Sangama:
Head: Nakkirara
Location: Northern Madura
Important books: Paripadal, Paditraputra, Nedunthokei etc.

The Monuments of the Sultanat Period

Quwwat-ul-Islam	**Qutb-ud-din Aibeq**
Qutb Minar	Qutb-ud-din Aibeq and Iltutamish
Adhaai Din ka Jhopda	Qutb-ud-din Aibeq
Lal Mahal	Balban
Alai Darwaza	Ala-ud-din Khalji
Jamaatkhana Mosque	Ala-ud-din Khalji
The mausoleum of Sikandar Lodi	Ibrahim Lodi
Sultan Garhi	Iltutamish
Hoz-e-Shamshi	Iltutamish
Atrin ka Darwaza	Iltutamish
Hoz-e-Khas	Ala-ud-din Khalji
Tughalaqabad	Ghiys-ud-din Tughlaq
The fort of Adilabad	Muhammad bin Tughlaq
Jahanpanah Nagar	Muhammad bin Tughlaq
Firozshah Kotla	Firozshah Tughlaq
Khan-e-Jahaan Tomb of Telangani	Junashah
Octagonal Black Mosque	Firozshah Tughlaq

– **Rajendra I**

- The official language of Gupta govern-ment – **Sanskrit**
- Which period is considered as the golden age of Indian history – **Gupta period**
- The last ruler of Gupta dynasty – **Vishnu Gupta**
- The founder of Vardhan empire – **Pushyabhuti**
- The founder of Pushyabhuti dynasty – **Narvardhan**
- Harshvardhana shifted his capital from Thaneshwar to – **Kannouj**
- The feudal system of land grants was started by – **Harshvardhana**
- The Chinese traveller Hiuen-Tsang came to India during the reign of – **Harshvardhana (606-646 A. D)**
- The famous book written by Hiuen-Tsang – **Si-Yu-Ki**
- Who is known as the prince of travellers – **Hiuen-Tsang**
- Who is known as 'Moral Connoisseur' and 'Shakya Muni' – **Hiuen-Tsang**
- The court poet of Harshavardhana – **Banbhatt**
- Where did Pulkeshin II defeat Harshavardhana in the year 634 A. D – **at the bank of Narmada river**
- The city where Harshavardhana used to organize his religious assembly every fifth year – **Prayag**
- The land revenue demanded by state in the reign of Harshavardhana – **1/6th of total produce**

Pallava Dynasty

- The founder of Pallava dynasty – **Sinhvishnu**
- The captal of the Pallavas – **Kanchipuram (Tamil Nadu)**
- The statues of Natraja belong to – **The Chola period**
- The founder of Rashtrakuta dynasty – **Dantidurga**
- The capital of Rashtrakutas dynasty – **Manyakheta**
- The capital of the Chalukyas – **Vatapi**

Ancient Poets and Their Patrons

Bana Bhatt	Harshvardhan
Somdeva	Prithvi Raj Third
Chander Bardai	Prithvi Raj Chauhan
Badayuni	Akbar
Faizi	Akbar
Kali Das	Chandra Gupta II
Amir Khusrav	Ala-ud-Din Khilji
Abul Fazl	Akbar

Famous Foreign Travellers

Original Country	Time Period	Indian Ruler
Megasthenes (Greek)	305 B.C	ChandraGupta Mourya
Deimachus (Syria)	298 B.C	Bindusara
Fa Hien (China)	399 A.D	Chandra Gupta II
Hiuen-Tsang (China)	630 A.D	Harshavardhana
I-Tsing (China)	675 A.D	------
Marco Polo (Italy)	1288A.D	Kayal (Pandyadynasty)
Ibn Battuta (Morocco)	1333A.D	Muhammad-bin-Tughlaq

Sikh Gurus and Their Deeds

Time Period as Guru	Name of the Guru	Deeds
1469-1538 A.D	Guru Nanak Dev	Establishment of Sikh religion, composition of 'Adi Granth'
1538-1552 A.D	Guru Angad	Progenitor of Gurumukhi script
1552-1574 A.D	Guru Amardas	Establishment of 22 seats for propagation of Sikh religion
1574-1581 A.D	Guru Ramdas	Establishment of Amritsar (1577)
1581-1606 A.D	Guru Arjun Dev	Laid the foundation of Golden Temple, compilation of 'Guru Granth sahib'
1606-1645 A.D	Guru Hargovind Singh	Foundation of 'Akal Takht', converted the Sikhs into a martial community
1645-1664 A.D	Guru Har Rai	Participated in the Mughal succession wars
1661-1664 A.D	Guru Harkishan	Died young
1664-1675 A.D	Guru Tegh Bahadur	Hanged by Aurangzeb because the Guru refused to accept Islam
1675-1708 A.D	Guru Gobind Singh	Founder of 'Khalsa Military', the last Guru

During Medival Period

Year	Invader	Contemporaneous Indian Ruler
1221 A. D	Genghis Khan	Iltutamis
1245 A. D	Hasan Karloon and Kabir Khan	Ala-ud-din Masud Shah
1285 A. D	Timur Khan (Mongol)	Balban
1292 A. D	Abdulla Khan (Mongol)	Jala-ud-din Khalji
1297 A. D	Kadir Khan (Mongol)	La-ud-din Khalji
1298 A. D	Saldi Khan (Mongol)	La-ud-din Khalji
1299 A. D	Kutluj Khwaza (Mongol)	Ala-ud-din Khalji
1303 A. D	Targi Khan (Mongol)	Ala-ud-din Khalji
1305 A. D	Ali Begh and Trataak Khan (Mongol) Ala-ud-din Khalji	Hanged by Aurangzeb because the Guru refused to accept Islam
1306 A. D	Iqbal Manda and Kubak (Mongol)	Ala-ud-din Khalji
1327 A. D	Tarma Shiri (Mongol)	Muhammad Tughlaq
1398 A. D	Amit Timur (Samarqand)	Mahmud Tughlaq
1510 A. D	Albuquerque (Portuguese Commander)	Yusuf Adil Shah (Bijapur)
1526 A. D	Babur (Mughal)	Ibrahim Lodi

Delhi

1. Anangpal Tomar is considered to be the founder Delhi city.
2. New Delhi designed by Edwin Lutyens.
3. Delhi's ancient name was Yoginipur.
4. The British government declared Delhi as the capital of India in 1911, the capital was formally shifted to Delhi in January1912. Before this, during the period of British Kolkata (Calcutta) was the capital of India.

- The founder of Chalukyas of Kalyani – **Tailap II**
- The last ruler of Chola dynasty – **Rajendra III**
- Military rule was first practiced in India by – **The Greeks**
- The ancient kingdom famous for its naval power – **The Cholas**
- 'Local self-government' was a characteristic of the – **Chola Administration**
- The capital of Hoysala dynasty – **Dwarasamudra**
- The Huns attacked India during the reign of – **Samudragupta (in 455 A. D)**
- The first ruler of the Hunas – **Torman**
- The founder of Saiyyed dynasty – **Khizr Khan**
- The last ruler of Saiyyed dynasty – **Alauddin Alam Shah**
- The emperor who used to earn his living by sewing caps – **Nasir-ud-din Mahmud**
- Mihirkala was defeated by – **Yashovarman**
- Varahmihir was an – **Astrologer**
- The great ruler of Sangama period – **Kaarivkala**
- The meaning of 'Sangama' in Tamil language – **a congregation/concert of poets**
- The first and third Sangamas were organized at – **Madurai**
- The second Sangama was organized at – **Kapaadapuram (Alvai)**
- The head of first Sangama – **Agastya**

Delhi Sultanat	
Early Turk Sultans	**Regnal Period**
Slave Dynasty (Mamluk Dynasty)	1206-90
Qutb-ud-din Aibek	1206-10
Aram Shah	1210-11
Iltutamish	1211-36
Ruqn-ud-din Firoz	1236
Razia	1236-40
Muiz-ud-din Bahram Shah	1240-42
Ala-ud-din Masud Shah	1242-46
Nasir-ud-din Mahmood	1246-65
Ghiyas-ud-din Balban	1265-87
Muiz-ud-din Kaikubad	1287-90
Kaimoor	1290
Khilji Dynasty	**1290-1320**
Jalal ud din Firuz Khilji	1290-96
Alauddin Khilji	1296-1316
Mubarak Khilji	1316-20
Tuglaq Dynasty	**1320-1414**
Ghiya-ud-din Tuglaq	1320-25
Muhammad bin Tuglaq	1325-51
Firoz Shah Tuglaq	1351-88
Ghiya-ud-din Tuglaqq II	1388-89
Abu Bakr Shah	1389
Nasir-ud-din Mahmood Shah	1390-94
Nasir-ud-din Mahmood	1394-1412
Sayyid Dynasty	**1414-1451**
Khizr Khan	1414-21
Mubarak Shah	1421-34
Muhammad Shah	1434-45
Alam Shah	1445-1450
Lodi Dynasty	**1451-1526**
Bahlol Lodi	1451-1489
Sikander Lodi	1489-1517
Ibrahim Lodi	1517-1526

Medieval History (1206 to 1858 A.D)

- Jaziya tax was imposed by – **Muhammad-bin-Qasim**
- The first Muslim invader to attack India –**Muhammad-bin-Qasim (in 712 A.D)**
- Mahmud of Ghazni's attacked India – **17 times (first attack in 1001 A. D)**
- In the first battle of Tarain, Prithviraj Chouhan defeated– **Muhammad Ghori**
- In the second battle of Tarain, **Muhammad Ghori defeated – Prithviraj Chouhan**
- The invader who plundered the temple of Somnatha in 1025 – **Mahmud of Ghazni**
- Muhammad-bin-Tughlaq shifted his capital from Delhi to – **Daulatabad**
- The architectural style of two copulas has been used in – **the mausoleum of Sikandar Lodi**
- The founder of Lodi dynasty – **Behlol Lodi**
- Who constructed the mausoleum of Behlol Lodi – **Sikandar Lodi (tomb)**
- Timur the Lame attacked India in – **1398 A. D (during the reign of Nasi-ud-din Mahmud)**
- The founder of Jaunpur city – **Firoz Shah Tughlaq**
- The spiritual master of Amir Khusrau – **Nizam-ud-din Auliya**
- Who constructed the Char Minar of Hyderabad – **Kuli Kutub Shah (in 1591 A. D)**
- The founder of Chandela dynasty – **Nanhuk**
- Khajuraho temples were built by – **the Chandelas**
- The architectural style used in the construction of Khajuraho temples – **Nagar style**
- Astdiggaja (Eight Elders) were – **the high officials in the court of Krishna Deva Raya**
- Navratnas were – **nine prominent courtesans of Akbar**
- 'The Akbar of Kashmir' – **Jain-ul-Abedin**
- The Vrihadeshvara temple of Tanjore (Dravida style) was built by – **Chola ruler Rajraja 1st.**
- The four places where the ruler of Jaipur Raja Savai Jaisingh built Janta-Mantar – **Delhi, Ujjain, Jaipur and Mathura**
- The city that is known as the 'Shiraz of the East' – **Jaunpur**
- The battle of Talikota was fought in

Sufi Sects and Their Founders		
Sect	**Founder**	**Propagator in India**
Chishti	Abu Abdal Chishti	Khwaja Muin-ud-din Chishti
Suhravardi	Zia-ud-din Abuljiv	Baha-ud-din Jakariya
Kadiri	Abdul Kadir	Shah Niyamtullah
Naqshbandi	Baha-ud-din	Makhdum Jilani
Shattariya	Abdul Shattar	Khwaja Bakibillah

Books of the Mughal Periods

Writer	Book
Babur	Baburnamah
Gulbadan Beghum (step-sister of Humayun)	Humayun Namah
Haider Dughalat	Tarikh-i-Raseedi
Khondmir	Qanoon-i-Humayuni
Mullah Daud	Tarikh-i-Alfi
Abul Fazl	Akbarnamah (Aain-i-Akbari)
Badayuni	Muntkhab-ut-Tawarikh
Nizam-ud-din Ahmed	Tabqat-i-Akbari
Faizi	Akbarnamah
Kajnivi	Nafais-ul-Ma'asir
Abbas Khan Servani	Tohfa-i-Akbari
Jahangir, Motmid Khan	Tujuk-i-Jahangiri
Abdul hamid Lahori	Padshahnamah
Moh. Amir Kajnivi	Badshahnamah
Inayat Khan	Shah Jahan Namah
Kajim Shiraji	Alamgirnamah
Dara Shikoh	Mazma-ul-Bahrin
Mutsaid Khan	Maasir-i-Alamgiri

the year –**1565 A. D (between Vijayanagar and the Confederation of Bahmani kingdoms)**

- Mirabai was contemporaneous to – **Tulsidas**
- The last Nawaab of Awadh – **Wajid Ali Shah**
- Abul Fazl was killed by – **Vir Singh Bundela**
- The capital of Aawadh prior to Lucknow – **Faizabad**
- The birth year and place of Mirabai – **in the Kudki village of Medta around 1499 A. D**
- Rani Lakshmi Bai's opponent in her last battle – **General Hugh Rose**
- Who built 'Alai Darwaza' – **Ala-ud-din Khalji**
- Who built the Lingaraja temple of Bhubaneswar – **king Yayati Kesri of Kesari dynasty**
- The Slave dynasty (Saltanat period) was founded by – **Qutubuddin Aibaq in 1206 A. D**
- The first muslim ruler of Delhi

The Navratns (Nine Jewels) of Akbar's Court

1. Mullah Do Pyaza	2. Hakim Khan
3. Tansen	4. Todarmal
5. Birbal	6. Abul Fazl
7. Abdul Rahim Khankhana	
8.Raja Mansingh	9. Faizi

Famous Battles Fought by Akbar

The Second Battle of Panipat	1556 A. D
The Victory of Malwa	1561 A.D
Possession of Chunar	1561 A.D
Possession of Medta	1562 A.D
The Victory of Ranthambore	1569 A.D
The Victory of Gujrat	1571 A.D
The Victory of Bihar and Bengal	1574-76 A.D
The Battle of Haldi Ghati	1576 A.D
The Victory of Kabul	1581 A.D
The Victory of Kashmir	1586 A.D

- Qutbuddin Aibeq

- Qutbuddin Aibeq started the construction of Qutb Minar; the cons- truction was completed by – **Iltutamish**
- Qutb Minar was constructed in the memory of – **Bakhtiyar Kaki**
- Iqtadari system was introduced by – **Iltutamish**
- 'Iqta' military was organized by – **Iltutamish**
- The first Afghan ruler of Delhi – **Bahlol Lodhi**
- The official language of Delhi Saltanat – **Persian/Turkish**
- The last ruler of Delhi Saltanat – **Ibrahim Lodhi**
- Intelligence (Spy) Department was consolidated by – **Ala-ud-din Khalji**
- Silver coin 'Tanka' and bronze coin 'Jital' first issued by – **Iltutamish**
- The first Turkish ruler to issue pure Arabic coins – **Iltutamish**
- Changez Khan invaded India during the reign of – **Iltutamishsa**
- The mausoleum of Qutb-ud-din Aibeq is situated at – **Lahore**
- The birth name of Muhammad bin Tughlaq – **Juna Khan/Ulugh Khan**
- The token currency was first introduced in India by – **Muhammad bin Tughlaq**
- Ibn Battuta (Moroccan traveler) came to India during the reign of

Important Mughal Rulers and their Reign

Ruler	Regnal Period
Babur	1526-30 A.D
Humayun	1531-40A.D and 1555-56A.D
Akbar	1556-1605 A. D
Jahangir	1605-27 A. D
Shah Jahan	1628-58 A. D
Aurangzeb	1658-1707 A.D

European Travelers in India during Mughal Period

Mughal Emperor	European Travellers
Akbar	Father Rufolf Acquaviva (1578), Father Antony Monserrate (1580-82), Ralph Fitch (1588-91),
Jahangir	William Hawkins (1603-13), William Fitch (1608), John Jourdian (1608-17), Nicholas Downton (1614), Nicholas Withington (1612-1616), Thomas Coryat (1612-17), Jacques 1st (1615), Sir Thomas Roe (1615-19), Edward Harry (1616-19), Petra Della Valle, Francisco Pelsaert
Shah Jahan	Baptist Tavernier, Francis Bernier
Aurangzeb	Francis Bernier, Jean de Thevenot (1666)

– Muhammad bin Tughlaq

- Meenakshi temple is situated at **– Madurai**
- The statue of Gommateshvara is situated in **– Karnataka**
- Hammurabi was the ruler of **– Babylon**
- The Treaty of Alinagar was signed in the year **– 1757 A.D**
- Dagh (branding of horses) and Huliya (descriptive roll) system was introduced by **– ala-ud-din Khilji**
- 'Market Control Policy' was introduced by **– Ala-ud-din Khilji**
- The policy of Blood and Iron followed by **– Balban**
- The real name of Balban was **– Baha-ud-din**
- The Theory of Kingship propounded by **– Balban**

Some Important Decisions Made by Akbar

Decision	Year
The abolition of slavery	1562
Akbar's emancipation from the grip of Harem clique	1562
The abolition of pilgrimage tax	1563
The abolition Jaziya tax	1564
The foundation of Fatehpur Sikri and the transfer of Capital from Delhi to Fatehpur Sikri	1571
The establishment of Ibadatkhana	1575
Allowed people's entrance	1578
The issuing of Mehzarnamah	1579
The establishment of Din-i-Ilahi	1582
The beginning of Ilahi calendar	1583
Transferring the capital to Lahore	1585

Special:

1. Akbar adopted Persian as the language of administration.
2. Akbar's first Vizier/Diwan/Finance Minister was Muzaffar Khan. His most famous and efficient finance minister was Todarmal.

The Attack of Nadir Shah

- Nadir Shah, the emperor of Iran, attacked India in 1739 A.D during the reign of Muhammad Shah.
- He returned to Iran carrying the wealths from India worth 70 crore rupees, he also took with him the Shah Jahan's throne Takh-i-Taus and Kohinoor diamond.

- The background for Bhakti movement was prepared by **– Ramanujacharya**

South India

- The first capital of Vijayanagara empire **– Hampi**
- The second capital of Vijanayagara empire **– Penukonda**
- The Vijayanagara empire established in the year **– 1336 A. D by two brothers Harihar and Bukka**
- Hampi is the residue of **– Vijayanagara empire**
- Hampi is located at the bank of river **– Tungbhadra**
- The Vijayanagara empire was established during the reign of which Sultan of Delhi **– Muhammad bin Tuglaq**
- The Kulguru (family master/teacher) of Krishna Deva Raya **– Vyasa Raj**
- Aurangzeb imprisoned Shivaji at **- Jaipur Bhavan (Agra)**
- The ruler also known as 'Andhra Bhoj' **– Krishna Deva Raya**
- Vitthala temple was built by **– Krishna Deva Raya**
- Golconda is located at

The Mausoleums of Famous Rulers

Ruler	Mausoleum
Babur	Kabul
Akbar	Sikandara
Jahangir	Lahore
Aurangzeb	Khuldabad
Humayun	Delhi
Sher Shah	Sasaram
Shah Jahan	Agra
Bahadur Shah Zafar	Rangoon(Yangon)

– **Hyderabad (Andhra Pradesh)**

- Hampi is located at – **Bellari (Karnataka)**
- Ahmednagar was merged in the year – **1632 A. D**
- Bhagat Singh, Rajguru and Sukhdeva were hanged on – **23rd March, 1931**
- The statue of Gomteshwara (Kaarnataka) was built by – **Chamund Raya**
- The battle of Wandiwash happened in the year – **1760 A. D (between the French and the British)**
- A famous Tat Mandir (Shore temple) – **Mamallapuram**
- Natraja temple is located at – **Chennai**
- The founder of Bahmani kingdom – **Ala-ud-din**
- When did Haider Ali die – **1782 A. D** (during the Second Anglo-**Mysore war)**
- The general famously known as 'Hazar Dinari' – **Malik Kafur**
- The last ruler of Slave Dynasty – **Sham- ud-din Kaimoor**
- The real name of Sher Shah – **Fareed Khan**
- The postal system was introduced by – **Sher Shah**
- The mausoleum of Sher Shah is located at – **Sasaram**
- Sher Shah Suri died at – **Kalinjar**
- Tipu Sultan was the ruler of – **Mysore (Karnataka)**
- The capital of Tipu Sultan – **Srirangapatnam**
- When did Tipu Sultan die – **1799 A. D** (during the Fourth Anglo-Mysore war)
- The 'Tree of Liberty' was planted at Srirangapatna by – **Tipu Sultan**
- The capital of Bahmani kingdom – **Gulbarga**
- The last ruler of Bahmani kingdom – **Kalimullah**
- Saint Tukaram was the contemporary of – **Jahangir**
- The coin 'anna' was introduced by – **Shah Jahan**

Mughal Period

- The Rupee coin was first minted in India during the reign of – **Sher Shah Suri**
- The last ruler of Tuglaq dynasty – **Nasir-ud-din Mahmood Shah Tuglaq**
- The first country to attack India during Mughal period – **Iran**

European Companies

Company	Year of Establishment
Portuguese East India Company	1498
British East India Company	1600
Dutch East India Company	1602
Danish East India Company	1616
French East India Company	1664
Swedish East India Company	1731

- Sufi sects emerged and developed during – **the 9th century A. D**
- The founder of Mughal dynasty – **Babur**
- The correct chronological order of the Mughal rulers is – **Babur, Humayun, Akbar, Jahangir, Shah Jahan, Aurangzeb**
- The full name of Babur – **Zahir-ud-din Muhammad Babur**
- The birth date of Babur – **24rd February, 1483 (in Fergana)**
- The full name of Humayun – **Nasir-ud-din Huamyun**
- Humayun came to throne in the year – **1530 A. D**
- The names of Humayun's brothers who challenged his right to throne – **Kamran, Hindal and Askari (along with the Afghans)**
- The 'Mausoleum of Bibi' is dedicated to the memory of – **Rabia-ud-Daurani (the first wife of Aurangzeb)**
- The first ruler to bring Brahmans under the Jaziya tax– **Firoz Shah Tuglaq**
- Babur died on– **27th December, 1530**
- The battle of Khanwa in 1527 was faught between- **Babur and Rana Sanga**
- Baburnamah was written by – **Babur (in Turkish language)**
- Who invited Babur to invade India – **Daulat Khan Lodi and Alam Shah**
- What was the chief reason of Babur's victory over Ibrahim Lodi (used for the first time in India) – **artillery**
- Tajmahal was constructed during the years – **1632-52 A. D**
- The battle of Plassey was fought between – **Siraj-ud-Daula and the British on 23rd June, 1757**
- The commander of British army in the battle of Plassey – **Lord Clive**
- Plassey is located in – **West Bengal**
- In the First battle of Panipat (1526 A. D) Babur defeated – **Ibrahim Lodi**
- In the Second battle of Panipat (5th November, 1556) Akbar defeated – **Hemu**
- In the Third battle of Panipat (1761

A. D) Ahmed Shah Abdali defeated – **the Marathas**

- Who led the Mughal army in the Second battle of Panipat – **Bairam Khan**
- The mausoleum of Jahangir was built by – **Noor Jahan**
- The childhood name of Ala –ud-din Khilji – **Ali and Gurshasp**
- The name of commander of Ala-ud-din Khilji – **Malik Kafur**
- The 'Do-Aspa' and 'Si-Aspa' Mansabs were introduced by – **Jahangir**
- When and where was Akbar born – **on 15th October, 1542 at Amarkot (Pakistan)**
- Akbar's coronation – **14th February, 1556 A. D at Kalanour fort (Punjab)**·
- Plassey is located in – West Bengal
- In the First battle of Panipat (1526 A. D) Babur defeated – **Ibrahim Lodi**
- In the Second battle of Panipat (5th November, 1556) Akbar defeated– **Hemu**
- In the Third battle of Panipat 1761 A. D) Ahmed Shah Abdali defeated – **the Marathas**

- Who led the Mughal army in the Second battle of Panipat – **Bairam Khan**
- The mausoleum of Jahangir was built by – **Noor Jahan**
- The childhood name of Ala –ud-din Khilji – **Ali and Gurshasp**
- The name of commander of Ala-ud-din Khilji – **Malik Kafur**
- The 'Do-Aspa' and 'Si-Aspa' Mansabs were introduced by– **Jahangir**
- When and where was Akbar born– **on 15th October, 1542 at Amarkot (Pakistan)**
- Akbar's coronation – **14th February, 1556 A. D at Kalanour fort (Punjab)**

- The name of Akbar's mother – **Hamida Banu**
- Akbar conferred the title 'Jadi Kalam' to – **Muhammad Hussain Kashmiri**
- Akbar conferred the title of 'Shirin Kalam' to – **Abdussamad**

The Incident of Chori-Choura

This event happened: on 5th February, 1922 in the Chori-Choura village of Gorakhpur district of the then United Provinces.

On this day: the crowd participating in the Non Cooperation movement turned violent.

The cause of the violence: the local S. H. O had beaten the people participating in the movement.

Result: the police fired at the protestors. The mob turned violent. At first they pelted the police office. Then they set the police station on fire and killed the S. H. O.

Casualty: according to the government report, three protesters and 23 policemen were killed in that incident.

Reaction: Gandhi was hurt by the violence and he revoked the movement.

- The most secular-minded Mughal ruler – **Akbar**
- The first British to come to Akbar's court – **Ralph Fitch**
- The battle of Haldi Ghati (18th June, 1576) was fought between – **Akbar and Maha Rana Pratap**
- Akbar was buried at – **Sikandara**
- The guardian of Akbar–**Bairam Khan**
- The official language of the Mughal administration – **Persian**
- The Buland Darwaza of Fatehpur Sikri was built by – **Akbar, in 1572 A. D (to celebrate Akbar's victory over Gujrat)**
- Baz Bahadur was the ruler of – **Malwa**
- Akbar conquered Chittor in the year – **1567 A. D**
- The author of 'Sir-i-Akbar'–**Dara Shikoh**
- Tulsidas was contemporaneous to – **Akbar**
- Akbar abolished slavery in the year – **1562**
- Mansabdari system was introduced by – **Akbar**
- Akbar started his Din-i-Ilahi or Tauhid-i-Ilahi religion in the year– **1582**
- The real name of Birbal was

Some Important Centers of the Revolution of 1857

Center	Leader	Date	British Adversary	Date of the Vanquishing
Delhi	Bakht Khan (military leader)	11-12th May, 1857	Nicholas and Hudson	21st Sept, 1857
Kanpur	Nana Sahib, Tantya Tope	5th June, 1857	Campbell	6th Sept, 1857
Lucknow	Begham Hazrat Mahal	4th June, 1857	Campbell	March, 1858
Jhansi	Rani Lakshmi Bai	June, 1857	Hugh Rose	3rd April, 1858
Allahabad	Liyakat Ali	1857	Colonel Neil	1858
Jagdishpur	Kunwar Singh	August, 1857	Vincent Eyre	1858
Bareli	Khan Bahadur Khan	1857	—	1858
Faizabad	Moulavi Ahmedullah	1857	—	1858
Fatehpur	Azimullah	1857	General Reynard	1858

Sessions of the Indian National Congress

Year	Location	President
1885	Bombay	Byomesh Chanda Banerjee (first president)
1886	Calcutta	Dada Bhai Nouroji
1887	Madras	Badruddin Taiyabji (first Muslim president)
1888	Allahabad	George Yule
1889	Bombay	William Wedderburn
1890	Calcutta	Firoz Shah Mehta
1891	Nagpur	V. Anand Charlu
1892	Allahabad	Byomesh Chandra Banerjee
1893	Lahore	Dadabhai Nouroji
1894	Madras	Alfred Webb (the making of the constitution of Congress)
1895	Pune	Surendranath Banerjee
1896	Calcutta	Rahimtullah Sayani (Vande Matram was sung in the Congress session for the first time)
1897	Amravati	Shankaran Nayar
1898	Madras	Anand Mohan Basu
1899	Lucknow	Ramesh Chandra Dutta
1900	Lahore	Narayan Ganesh Chandavarkar
1901	Calcutta	Dinshaw Eduljee Wacha
1902	Ahmedabad	Surendra nath Banerjee
1903	Madras	Lal Mohan Ghosh
1904	Bombay	Sir Henry Cotton
1905	Banaras	Gopal Krishna Gokhle
1906	Calcutta	Dada Bhai Nouroji (the term Swaraj was used for the first time)
1907	Surat	Ras Bihari Bose
1908	Madras	Ras Bihari Bose
1909	Lahore	Madan Mohan Malviya
1910	Allahabad	William Wedderburn
1911	Calcutta	Bishan Narayan Dutta (Jan-Gan-Man was sung for the first time)
1912	Bankipur	R.B Rangnath Nrisingh
1913	Karachi	Nawab sayyid Muhammad Bahadur
1914	Madras	Bhupendra Nath Basu
1915	Bombay	Satyendra Prasad Sinha
1916	Lucknow	Ambika Charan Majumdar (alliance with the Muslim League)
1917	Calcutta	Ani Besant (first woman president)
1918	Delhi	Madan Mohan Malviya
1919	Amritsar	Moti Lal Nehru
1920	Nagpur	Chakravarti Vijaya Raghavacharya
1921	Calcutta	Hakim Azmal Khan (special session)
1922	Gaya	Chitranjan Das
1923	Delhi	Abul Kalam Azad (the youngest president)
1924	Belgaon	Gandhi (gandi became the president for the first time)
1925	Kanpur	Sarojini Naidu (first Indian woman president)
1928	Calcutta	Motilal Nehru
1929	Lahore	Jawahar Lal Nehru (the demand for Complete Self-Rule)
1931	Karachi	Sardar Patel
1932	Delhi	Ranchhodmal Amritlal
1933	Calcutta	Nelli Sengupta
1934	Bombay	Rajendra Prasad
1936	Calcutta	Jawagar Lal Nehru
1937	Faizpur	Jawahar Lal Nehru (the first session to be organized in a village)
1938	Haripura	Subhash Chandra Bose
1939	Tripura	Subhash Chandra Bose
1946	Meerut	J. B. Kriplani
1947	Delhi	Rajendra Prasad
1948	Jaipur	Pattabhi Sitaramaiya

– **Mahesh Das**

- Faizi and Birbal were – **the courtesans of Akbar**
- Tuglaq dynasty ended in the year – **1412**
- The first British to appear in the Mughal court – **William Hawkins (1608-11)**
- The famous (bird) painters at the time of Jahangir – **Ustad Mansoor and Abul Hasan**
- The real name of Mumtaj Mahal – **Arzumand Bnao Begham**
- The Red Fort and Jama Masjid of Delhi were built by – **Shah Jahan**
- Shah Jahan was born on – **5th January, 1592, in Lahore**
- The childhood name of Shah Jahan – **Khurram**
- Shah Jahan's mother's name –**Jagat Gosain**
- Aurangzeb kept shah janha under house arrest at the– **Red Fort in Agra.**
- Who built the Jama Masjid in the Agra Red Fort – **Jahan Ara Begham**
- Who built the Moti Masjid in the Red Fort of Delhi – **Aurangzeb**
- The mausoleum of Tansen is located at – **Gwalior**
- The first teacher of Tansen – **Muhammad Gous**
- The author of 'Humayun Namah' – **Gulbadan Begham**
- The 'jihad' started by Aurangzeb means – **Dar-ul-Islami**

All India Muslim League

Foundation: 30th December, 1906, the resolution was passed during Dhaka session.
Dissolution: 14th August, 1947; it was replaced with Muslim League.
Headquarter: Lucknow
Main objective: The concept of two different states for Hindus and Muslims. The aim of carving out a different country for the Muslims.
Initial leadership: Sir, Saiyyed Ahmed Khan, Mohammad Ali Jinnah, Liyakat Ali Khan

- The Baburi mosque of Ayodhya was built by – **Mir Baqi (the commander of Babur)**
- The 'Panchmahal' of Fatehpur Sikari was built by – **Akbar**
- The foundation of Agra city was laid in 1504 A. D by – **Sikandar Lodi**
- Baburnamah was translated in Persian by– **Abdul Rahim Khan-i-Khana**
- The full name of Humayun – **Nasiruddin Humayun**
- The ruler who believed in astronomy – **Humayun**
- Who introduced the rule to wear clothes of a specific color on each day of the week – **Humayun**
- To whom did Sher Khan (Sher Shah) defeat in the battle of Chousa on 25th June, 1539 – **Humayun**
- Humayun tomb was constructed under the supervision of– **Akbar's step-mother Haji Begham**
- The architect of Humayu's tomb - **Mirak Mirza Gyas**
- The mausoleum of Jahangir is located at – **Shahdara Bagh, Lahore**
- The childhood name of Jahangir – **Salim**
- 'Zanjir-i-Adl' (the Chain of Justice) was installed by – **Jahangir**
- The British East India Company who attended the court of Jahangir – **William Hawkins (in 1608 A. D, Jahangir used to call him 'English Khan')**
- The diamond fitted at the Peacock Throne – **Kohinoor**
- The last Mughal ruler to sit on the Peacock throne – **Muhammad Shah**
- The architect of the Peacock throne – **Bebadal Khan**
- Mughal emperor is known as 'Zinda Pir' – **Aurangzeb**
- The Mughal ruler who went through coronation twice –**Aurangzeb**
- Treaty of Purandar was signed in 1665 between– **Shivaji and Jai Singh**
- Aurangzeb was cremated at– **Daulatabad**

Modern History (1850 to Present)

- The First Karnataka war was fought in 1746 A. D between – **the French and the British**
- The eliminator of Pindaris–**Lord Hastings**
- Gandhi-Irwin Pact was signed in the year – **1931**
- The foundation of 'Anushilan Samiti' – **by Barindra Ghosh and Bhupendra Nath Dutt (in 1907, in Kolkata)**

Indian National Congress

Foundation	28-31 Dec,1885
Founder	A.O. Hume
Foundation venue	Gokuldas Tejpal Women's Sanskrit College, Bombay
First president	Byomesh Chandra Banerjee
Total number of delegates	72
The Prime Minister of Britain at the time of the first session	Gladstone
The leader who did not participate in the first session	Surendra Nath Banerjee
The first Muslim president of the Congress	Badruddin Taiyabji
The first European president of the Congress	George Yule
The first woman president of the Congress	Annie Besant
The first Indian woman president of the Congress	Sarojini Naidu
The first woman to address the Congress	Kadambini Ganguly
The president of the Congress at the time of the Independence	J. B. Kriplani

- The policy of Dual Rule was abolished by– **Waren Hastings (in 1772)**
- The last Mughal ruler – **Bahadur Shah Zafar**
- Who was known as 'Shah-i-Bekhabar' – **Bahadur Shah 1st.**

The Marathas

- The Maratha kingdom was established by – **Shivaji**
- Who is considered the second founder of Maratha kingdom – **Peshwa Balaji Vishwanath**
- The spiritual master of Shivaji – **Guru Ramdas**
- The name of Shivaji's infantry and the land revenue system – **Paik and Raiyatbadi respectively**
- The real name of Tantya Tope – **Ramchandra Pandurang**
- The cabinet of Shivaji was known as – **Ashtpradhan**
- The highest post in the Ashtpradhan – **Peshwa**
- Then Shivaji was crowned as the king of the Marathas by - **Ganga Bhatt (a Pandit from Kashi) at the Raigadh fort**
- What were the 'Chouth' and 'Sardeshmukhi' during the time of Shivaji – **taxes**
- The first (Maratha) ruler to accept the Subsidiary Alliance – **Peshwa Bajirao II**
- Who is known as the 'contemptuous coward' of the Mughal dynasty

Some Important Court Cases against Indian Revolutionaries

Nasik Conspiracy Case	1909-10	Vinayak Savarkar was expatriated,other 26 were imprisoned
Alipur or Maniktalla Conspiracy Case	1908	Arbindo Ghosh and many others were tried
Howrah Conspiracy Case	1910	Jatin Mukherjee was the main accused
Dhaka Conspiracy Case	1910	Pulin Das was sentenced to 7 years imprisonment
Delhi Conspiracy Case	1912	Master Ameen Chandra, Awadh Bihari and Bal Mukunda were sentenced to death
Banaras Conspiracy Case	1915-16	Sachindra Sanyal was sentenced life imprisonment at Kala Pani
Kakori Conspiracy Case	1925	Thakur Roshan singh,Rajendranath Lahiri,Ramprasad Bismil and Ashfaqullah Khan were sentenced to death

– **Farrukhsiyar**

Sikh History

- The compiler of 'Adi Grantha' – **Guru Arjundev**
- Thr Golden Temple at Amritsar was built by – **Guru Arjundev**
- The land for the Golden Temple was donated by – **Akbar**
- The gold coated dome of the Golden Temple was donated by – **Maharaja Ranjit Singh**
- The architect of the Golden Temple – **Mian Mir**
- Gurumukhi script was invented by – **Guru Angad**
- The founder of the Akal Takht – **Guru Hargovind Singh**
- The birth year and place of Guru Nanak Dev – **1469 A. D, Talwandi**
- The birth year and place of Guru Govind Singh – **1666 A. D, Patna Sahib (Patna)**
- Guru Govind Singh was murdered at – **Nanded (Maharashtra) in the year 1708 A. D**

Some Major Revolts Against the British Rule

Movement/ Revolt	Leader	Year
Sanyasi revolt	Kena Sarkar, Dirji Narayan	1763-1800
Chuar revolt	Durjan Singh	1798
Veluthampi revolt	Veluthampi	1808-09
Bhil revolt	Seva Ram	1825-31
Ramose revolt	Chittar Singh	1822-29
Pagalpanthi revolt	Tipu	1825-27
Ahom revolt	Gomdhar Kunwar	1828
Wahabi movement	Saiyyed Ahmed Titumir	1831
Kol revolt	Narayan Rao	1831-32
Khasi revolt	Tirath Singh	1833
Fairazi movement	Shaiatullah	1839
Santhal revolt	Siddhu Kanhu	1855-57
Munda revolt	Birsa Munda	1899-1900
Neel movement	Digambar	1859-60
Pabna revolt	Ishan Chandra Roy, Shambhupal	1873-76
Mopla revolt	Ali Mudaliar	1920-22
Koka movement	Bhagat Jawahar Lal	—
Rampa revolt	Sitaram Raju	1879-1922
Tana Bhagat movement	Jatra Bhagat	1914
Tebhaga movement	Kamparam Singh, Bhawan Singh	1946
Telangana movement	–	1946

Important Revolutionary Events

Year	Incident	Location	Revolutionaries
1897	The murder of Commissioner Rand and Elmhurst	Pune	Chapekar Brothers
1908	The attempt to assassi-nate Kingsford (Alipur Conspiracy Case)	Muzaffar pur	Khudiram Bos, Prafful Chaki
1909	Jackson murder	Nasik	Anant Kanhere
1909	Colonel Wiley murder	London	Madan Lal Dhingra
1912	The attempt to assassinate Viceroy Harding (Delhi Bomb Conspiracy)	Delhi	Ras Bihari Bose,Basant Kumar
1927	Kakori Conspiracy	Kakori	Ram Prasad Bismil, Ashfaqullah Khan
1928	The assassination of Sanders	Lahore	Sardar Bhagat Singh
1930	Armory robbery incident	Chatgaon	Suryasen
1940	The assassination of Michael O'Dwyer	London	Udham Singh

- The 5th sikh guru Guru Arjun Dev was hanged on order of – **Jahangir**
- The author of Tuglaq Namah – **Amir Khusrau**
- Who killed the ninth guru of the Sikhs Guru Tegh Bahadur – **Aurangzeb (because the Guru refused to convert to Islam)**
- The founder of the Khalsa Panth – **Guru Govind Singh, in the year 1699 A. D**
- Who is known as 'The Mother of the Indian Revolution' – **Bhikaji Rustam Kama**

The Revolution of 1857

- The revolution of 1857 started at – **Meerut (10th May, 1857)**
- Who was the Mughal emperor at the time of the revolution of 1857? – **Bahadur Shah Zafar II**
- Who termed the revolt of 1857 as 'the first freedom struggle of India? – **Vir Savarkar**
- The insignia of the revolution of 1857 were – **lotus and bread**
- Who was the Prime Minister of Britain at the time of the revolution of 1857 – **Lord Palmerston**
- Who called the revolt of 1857 the 'national revolt'– **Benjamin Disraeli**
- Who was the Governor-general of India during the revolt of 1857 – **Lord Canning**
- Who led the revolt of 1857 in Bihar – **Vir Kunvar Singh (the zamindar of Jagdishpur)**
- The Urdu poet who witnessed the revolt of 1857 – **Mirza Ghalib**
- The Kakori Train Conspiracy happened on – **9th August, 1925**
- The Jalianwala Bagh massacre happened on – **13th April 1919 (Viceroy of India was Lord Chelmsford**
- The commission appointed to investigate the Jalianwala Bagh massacre – **Hunter Commission**
- The partition of Bengal happened on **– 16th October, 1905 (by Lord Curzon)**·
- When was the partition of Bengal cancelled – **in 1911, by Lord Harding**
- Captain Hawkins visited the court of – **Jahangir**
- The first French governor – **Duplex**

Some Important Quotes, Slogans and Songs Related to the Freedom Struggle of India

Famous Slogan/Quote/Song	Related Person
Swaraj is my birthright	Bal Gangadhar Tilak
Sarfaroshi ki tamanna ab hamaaredil me hai	Ram Prasad Bismil
India was won through sword and it shall be ruled through sword	Lord Elgin
Sare jahan se achchha Hindostan hamara	Allama Iqbal
Vande Matram	Bankim Chandra Chaterjee
He Ram	Mahatma Gandhi
Jan-Gan-Man Adhinayak Jai He	Rabindra Nath Tagore
Who lives if India dies	Jawahar Lal Nehru
Inqalab Zindabad	Mohammed Iqbal
Dilli Chalo	Subhash Chandra Bose
We begged for bread, but we were given stones (while starting Civil Disobedience Movement)	Mahatma Ghandi,
A post-dated check drawn on a crashing bank	Mahatma Gandhi with reference to the Cripps Mission
The whole India has been turned Into a prison	C R. Das
The blows struck at me today will be last nails in the coffin of the British rule in India	Lala Lajpat Rai
Total Self-rule	Jawahar Lal Nehru
Hindi, Hindu, Hindostan	Bhartendu Harishchandra
Give me your blood and I shall give you your freedom	Subhash Chandra Bose
Return to the Vedas	Dayanand Saraswati
Aram Haram Hai (leisure leads to doom)	Jawahar Lal Nehru
Quit India	Mahatma Gandhi
Vijayi Vishwa Tiranga Pyara	Shyam Lal Gupta
Do or Die	Mahatma Gandhi
Jai Hind	Subhash Chandra Bose

Some Important Battles in Indian History		
War	**Date/ Year**	**The Warring Sides**
The battle of Jhelum/Vitasta	326 B. C	Alexander and Porus
The first battle of Tarain	1191	Muhammed Ghori and Prithivi Raj Chouhan
The second battle of Tarain	1192	Muhammed Ghori and Prithvi Raj Chouhan
The battle of Chandawar	1194	Muhammed Ghori and Raja Jaichand
The first battle of Panipat	1526	Babur and Ibrahim Lodi
The battle of Khanwa	1527	Babur and Rana Sanga
The battle of Chanderi	1528	Babur and Medini Rai
The battle of Chousa	1529	Humayun and Sher Shah Suri
The battle of Ghaghra	1539	Humayun and the Afghans
The battle of Bilgram	1540	Humayun and Sher Shah Suri
The second battle of Panipat	1556	Akbar and Hemu
The battle of Talikota	1565	Bahmani and Vijayanagara kingdoms
The battle of Haldi Ghati	1576	Akbar and Rana Pratap
The battle of Asirgadh	1599-1600	Akbar and Miran Bahadur
The battle of Karnal	1739	Nadir Shah and the Mughal ruler Muhammad Shah
The battle of Plassey	1757	Robert Clive and Sirajuddoula
The battle of Wandiwansh	1760	The British and the French
The third battle of Panipat	1761	Ahmed Shah Abdali and the Marathas
The battle of Buxar	1764	The British and the joint army of three Indian rulers
The first Mysore war	1767-69	Haider Ali and the British
The second Mysore war	1780-84	Haider Ali and the British
The third Mysore war	1790	Tipu Sultan and the British
The fourth Mysore war	1799	Tipu Sultan and the British
The battle of Chilian	1849	The British and the Sikhs
India-China border war	1962	India and China
Indo-Pak war	1965	India and Pakistan
Indo-Pak war	1971	India and Pakistan
Kargil war	1999	India and Pakistan

- In which year did Sir Thomas Roe came to the court of Jahangir – **1615**
- The incident of Black Hole happened in the year – **1756**
- The Mughal ruler who participated in the battle of Buxar (1764)–**Shah Alam 2nd**
- Who was the commander of British troops in the battle of Buxar – **Major Hector Munro**
- Who was known as the 'Hermit of Shimla' – **A. O. Hume (resident of Scotland)**
- The battle of Buxar was fought between – **Mir Qasim, Shirajuddoula and Shah Alam on the one side and the British on the other side·**
- The Treaty of Allahabad happened in the year – **1765**
- The Congress was founded on – **28th December, 1885 (Lord Dufferin was the Viceroy of India)**
- The founder of the Congress – **A. O. Hume·**
- Who was the head of the first session of the Congress (Bombay, 1885) – **Byomesh Chandra Banerjee**
- In what session did the Congress had to face division among its members – **Surat session, 1907**
- The Moderate and the Extremist factions of the Congress rejoined in what session–**Lucknow session, 1916**
- Who was the Viceroy of India during the Surat Split – **Lord Minto**
- Mahatma Gandhi was elected the president of Congress in what session – **Belgaon session (1924, Karnataka)**
- Gandhi went to South Africa in the year – **1893**
- Gandhi came back to India from South Africa in the year – **1915**
- Gandhi established the Sabarmati ashram in the year – **1916**
- The first British president of the Congress – **George Yule**

- The first Muslim president of the Congress – **Badruddin Taiyabji**
- Swadeshi movement was started in the year – **1905**
- The Muslim League passed the Pakistan resolution in – **the Lahore session (1940)**
- The inventor of the word 'Pakistan' – **Choudhary Rahmat Ali**
- The first prime minister of Pakistan – **Liyakat Ali**
- The motion of 'Total Independence' was passed in what session of the Congress – **Lahore session (1929)**
- Who made the announcement about the independence of India – **Clement Attlee (the British prime minister)**
- The Gadar Party was established in the year – **1913, in San Francisco by Lala Hardayal**
- The initiator of Home Rule movement – **Anne Besant**
- Which act was known as 'the Black Act' – **Rowlett Act** ·
- Rowlett act was passed in the year – **1919**
- Who called Gandhi 'the Naked Fakeer' – **Winston Churchill**
- Who addressed Gandhi as 'the father of the nation' (Rashtrapita) for the first time – **Subhash Chandra Bose (from Rangoon Radio)**
- The first Satyagraha started by Gandhi in India – **Champaran Satyagraha (in 1917)**
- The British East India Company came to India in the year – **1600**
- Simon Commission came to India in the year – **1928**
- The Cripps Mission came to India in the year – **1942**
- The head of the Cabinet Mission – **Lord Pethick-Lawrence**
- Who said – 'Nehru is a patriot whereas Jinnah is a politician' – **Moulana Azad**
- Which European nationals first came to India – **the Portuguese**
- Who was the first Portuguese merchant to come to India – **Vasco da Gama (came to Calicut in 1498)**
- Vasco da Gama came to India for the second time in the year – **1502**
- Who consolidated the Portuguese power-hold in India – **Albuquerque**
- Where did the Portuguese establish their first factory (fort) – **Cochin (1503)**
- When did the Portuguese won Goa – **1510**
- With whose permission did the British establish their first factory in Surat in the year 1608 – **Jahangir**
- Who was the first Portuguese Governor in India – **Francisco da Almeida, 1505 A. D**
- The chronological order of the arrival of the Europeans in India – **Portuguese, Dutch, British, Danish, French, Swedish**
- The first Briton to come to India – **Milden Hall**
- Who abolished the practice of Sati – **Lord William Bentinck (in 1829 A. D)**
- Who gave the theory of the 'Drainage of Wealth' (1867)–**Dadabhai Nouroji**
- Whose slogan is 'India is for the Indians' – **Arya Samaj**
- Who prepared the designs of the Tajmahal–**Ustad Isha Khan (Persian)**
- The Gateway of India was built in the year – **1924**
- India Gate was built in the year– **1921**
- Prince of Wales visited India – **1921**
- The capital of India was transferred from Calcutta to Delhi in the year – **1912 (Lord Harding II was the Viceroy of india)**
- Who envisioned the 'Azad Hind Fouj' – **Captaiin Mohan Singh**
- Who was the founder of 'Azad Hind Fouj' – **Ras Bihari Bose (1942)**
- The founder of 'Azad Hind Government' – **Subhash Chandra Bose (23rd October, 1943)**
- Who designed the flag of independent India – **Pingali Venkayya**
- The first Round Table Conference was organized on the date – **12th November, 1930 (London)**
- Who inaugurated the first Round Table Conference– **King George 5th**
- Who was the chairman of the first Round Table Conference – **Prime Minister Ramsay McDonald**
- Who was the Viceroy of India during the first Round table Conference – **lord Irwin**
- The second Round Table Conference was held – **in 1931 (London)**
- Who was the sole representative of the Congress at the second Round Table Conference–**Mahatma Gandhi**
- Tirupati temple is located in – **Andhra Pradesh**
- Who was the proponent of 'Open Door Policy' – **John Hay**

- When was the Swaraj party established – **in 1923**
- The central tenet of the Brahmo Samaj was – **monotheism**
- Slavery was outlawed in the year – **1843**
- Vernacular Act was passed in the year – **1878 (by Lord Litton)**
- Vernacular Press Act was annulled in the year – **1882 (by Lord Ripon)**
- Who led the Ahom revolt – **Gomdhar Kunwar (1828, in Assam)**
- The calcutta Madarsah was establish by Warren Hastings – **in 1781**
- The famine of Bengal – **in 1770**
- The founder of Dual rule in Bengal – **Robert Clive**
- Who were the founders of Swaraj party – **Chitranjan Das and Motilal Nehru**
- The Buddhist philosopher to propagate the doctrine of zero/nothingness for the first time – **Nagarjuna**
- Best Bakery Massacre happened in which city – **Baroda (Gujrat)**
- Bhimbetka is famous–**for cave paintings**
- Ajanta and Ellora caves are located in – **Maharashtra**
- Who built the Angkor Wat temple of Cambodia – **the Cambodian ruler Suryavarman II**
- Munda tribal revolted during – **1899-1900 (Birsa Munda was their leader)**
- Where did the Mopla revolt of 1921 happen – **in Kerala**
- Who was elected as the 'permanent' member of the Muslim League in March 1908 – **Agha Khan**
- When was queen Victoria crowned as the queen of India – **in 1877**
- Who was the Viceroy of India at the start of the Non Cooperation movement – **Lord Chelmsford**
- Who established 'Abhinava Bharata' in 1904 at Nasik – **Vinayak Damodar Savarkar**
- Who started the Raiyatwadi system – **Holt Mackenzie**
- Who introduce Albert Act–**Lord Rippon**
- The Lee Commission was established in the year – **1924**
- Who translated the Bhagwat Gita into English language–**William Wilkins**
- The first state to sign Subsidiary Alliance – **Hyderabad**
- The August resolution was brought on the day – **8th August, 1940**
- Human sacrifice and female infanticide banned by–**Lord Harding**

World History

- Who gave the slogan 'One Czar, one Church and one Russia' – **Czar Nicholas II**
- Burma achieved independence on – **4th January 1948**
- When did the Glorious Revolution happen in England – **1688**
- The first president of the Republic of China – **Sun Yat Sen**
- Who is considered the builder of modern Russia – **Stalin**
- Who was the originator of Protestant religion – **Martin Luther (German)**
- To which country did the famous painter Pablo Picasso belong – **Spain**
- The slogan 'Equality, Liberty, Fraternity' was given by – **the French revolution**
- Napoleon became the emperor of France in the year – **1804 A. D**
- The name of Napoleon's father – **Carlo Bonaparte**
- Who is known as Messiah of nationalism – **Napoleon**
- How many countries participated in the first world war (1914-18) – **37**
- Which country had to bear the maximum losses in the first world war – **Germany**
- When did America involve in the first world war – **on 6th April, 1917**
- The American president at the time of the first world war–**Woodrow Wilson**
- The Viceroy of India at the time of the first world war – **Lord Harding II**
- The immediate reason behind the first world war–**the assassination of Austrian Crown-Prince Ferdinand in Sarajevo**
- The prime minister of Britain at the time of the second world war – **Winston Churchill**
- The president of USA at the time of the second world war – **Franklin D. Roosevelt**
- How many countries participated in the second world war – **61**
- The immediate reason for the second world war – **German attack on Poland**
- The last Axis country to accept the defeat in the second world war – **Japan**
- The Viceroys of India at time of the second world war – **Lord Linlithgow (at the beginning) and Lord Wavell at the end)**

INDIAN AND WORLD GEOGRAPHY

- The father of geography – **Hecataeus**
- The father of modern geography – **Alexander Von Humboldt**
- The father of organized geography – **Eratosthenes**
- The first user of the word – **'Geographica' Eratosthenes**
- The father of physical geography – **Polidoneum**
- The father of cultural geography – **Carl O. Sauer**
- The founders of mathematical geography – **Thales and Anaximander**
- The maker of the globe of the world – **Martin Behaim**
- The maker of the map of the world – **Anaximander**
- The author of Encyclopedia of Geography – **Strabo**

The Universe: A Comprehensive Introduction

- The sky that covers the earth is actually – **The universe**
- The study of the universe is known as – **Cosmology**
- The constant expansion of the universe is due to – **the Big Bang**
- The first scientist to put forward the theory of the Big Bang in relation to the creation of the universe – **George Lamaitre**
- The explosive star in the universe – **Supernova**
- The age of the universe has been estimated to be – **13 Billion years (130 Crore years)**
- The diameter of the universe – **10^8 Light Years**
- The distance traveled by light in an year is known as – **a Light Year**
- The biggest unit for measuring cosmic distances is – **Parsec**
- 1 Parsec is equal to – **3.26 Light Years**
- Light Year is a unit of – **distance**
- 1 Light Year is equal to – **9.46×10^{12} K. M or 9.46×10^{15} Meter**
- Who said that Sun was the center of the universe – **Copernicus**
- To which country did Copernicus belong – **Poland**
- Who said that sun is the center of the solar system – **Johannes Kepler**
- Who was the first scientist to declare that the earth was round shaped – **Pythagoras**
- The group of star clusters is known as – **Galaxy**
- The shape of the galaxies is – **Spiral**
- The diameter of our galaxy is – **10^5 Light Years**
- The beautiful pattern of the stars is known as a – **constellation**
- The total number of constellations is – **89**
- The biggest constellation is – **Hydra**
- The most sparkling constellation is – **Centaurus**
- Our closest neighboring galaxy is – **Andromeda**
- The average distance of an Astronomical Unit is – **the distance between the earth and the sun**
- The galaxy in which the earth and its solar system is located is known as – **The Milky Way galaxy**
- Milky Way is a – **galaxy**
- A galaxy is – **a cluster of millions of stars that appear blurry from the earth (because of their distance)**
- The newest discovered galaxy – **Dwarf galaxy**
- The Pulsars are – **the stars that rotate at high speed on their axis**
- Who saw the Milky way galaxy for the first time – **Galileo**
- The comet that appears after every 76 years – **Halley's comet**
- Halley's comet will reappear in the year – **2062 A. D**

The Sun	
Minimum distance from earth	14.70 Crore K. M
Maximum distance from earth	15.21 Crore K. M
The average distance from earth	14.98 Crore K. M
The diameter of the sun	13,92,200 K. M
The radius of the sun	6,96,100 K. M (110 times the radius of the earth)
Volume	13 Lakh time more than that of the earth's volume
Mass	3,32,000 times more than the mass of the earth

Photosphere (surface) temperature	6000° centigrade
The temperature of the core	15 million centigrade
Energy emission	Yule/Second
Rotation period	25.38 days (relative to the equator) and 33 days (relative to the poles)
Chemical composition	Hydrogen – 70%, Helium – 28.5% and other components 2%
Age	5 billion years approximately
How much time does the sunlight take to reach to earth from the sun	8 minutes and 18 seconds
The speed of the sunlight	Metre/Second (3 lakh K. M/second)

The Solar System: Some Important Facts

The biggest planet	Jupiter
The smallest planet	Mercury
The natural satellite of earth	Moon
The planet closest to the sun	Mercury
The planet farthest to the sun	Pluto
The planet closest to earth	Venus
The brightest planet	Venus
The planet with maximum natural satellites	Jupiter
The coldest planet	Pluto
The planet that appears red during night	Mars
The heaviest planet	Jupiter
The biggest natural satellite of the solar system	Ganymede
The smallest natural satellite of the solar system	Deimos
The blue planet	Earth
The red planet	Mars
The star of the twilight/daybreak	Venus
The sister of earth	Venus

The Planets

Planet	Duration of Revolve around the Sun	Duration of Rotatation on Their Axis	Number of the Satellites
Mercury	88 days	58.6 days	0
Venus	224.7 days	243 days	0
Earth	365.26 days	23.9 hours	1
Mars	687 days	24.6 hours	2
Jupiter	11.9 years	9.9 hours	63
Saturn	29.5 years	10.3 hours	60
Uranus	84.0 years	17.2 hours	27
Neptune	164.8 years	17.1 hours	13

The Galaxies

The Name of the Galaxy	Luminosity
The Milky Way	—
Large Magellanic Cloud	0.9
Small Magellanic Cloud	2.5
Ursa Minor System	—
Sculpture System	80
Draco System	—
Fornax System	8.3
Leo – 11 System	12.04
Leo – 1 System	12.0

The Earth

The estimated age of earth	4.6 billion years
Total surface area	51,01,00,500 square/ K. M
Land surface area (29.08%)	14,89,50,800 square/ K. M
Water surface area (70.92%)	36,11,49,700 square/ K. M
Average density	5.52 gram per cube centimeter
The Equatorial diameter	12,756 K. M
The Polar diameter	12,714 K. M
What speed is needed to escape earth's gravity	11.2 K. M/second
Mass	K. G
Volume	10,83,20,88,40,000 Cube K. M
The highest point from the sea level	8,848 meters (Mount Everest)
The lowest point from the sea level	11,033 meters (Mariana Trench, Pacific Ocean, east of Philippines)
The lowest point on the land	The Dead Sea (396 meters, Israel/ Jordon)
The earth takes to time complete one rotation on its axis	23 hours, 56 minutes, 40.91 seconds

The Composition of the Atmosphere

Sphere	Height (K. M)	Special Facts
Troposphere	0-18	All weather related changes happen in this zone.
Stratosphere	18-50	Wind blows, the Ozone layer is also situated in this layer
Mesosphere	50-80	The temperature falls as the height increases
Thermo sphere	80-640	This zone contains electrically charged particles. The radio waves return back to earth after hitting this layer
Exosphere	Above 640 K.M	Temperature is around 5000° C

The Moon

Distance from earth	3,82,200 K. M
Diameter	3,475 K. M
The mass of the moon in comparison to the mass of earth	1:8.1
The ration of the gravitational pull of the Moon and earth	1:6
The part of the moon's surface that remains unseen	41%
The maximum distance between moon and earth (apogee distance)	4,06,000 K. M
The minimum distance between moon and earth (perigee distance)	3,64,000 K. M
The time moon takes to revolve around the earth (rotation period)	27 days, 7 hours
The rotation period of moon (on its axis)	43 minutes, 11.47 seconds
The height of the highest mountain on the moon	35,000 feet (mount Leibniz, located at the south pole of the moon)
How much time does the light take to reach to earth from moon	1.3 seconds

Local Winds

Local Wind	Related Area
Foehn	The Alps mountains
Chinook	North America
Mistral	France
Sirocco	Sahara deserts
Berg	South Africa
Simum	Iran
Santa Ana	California
Loo	India-Pakistan

Water Distribution on the Earth

1.	Oceans	97.25%
2.	Glaciers	2.05%
2.	Underground water	0.68%
4.	Rivers and lakes	0.02%

The Transformation of Rocks

1. **Basic Rock**	**Transformed Rock**
2. Shale	Slate
3. Lime Stone	Marble
4. Chalk and Dolomite	Marble
5. Sand Stone	Quartz
6. Basalt	Cist
7. Slate	Phyllite
8. Conglomerate	Quartz

The Distribution of Gases in the Atmosphere

1. Nitrogen	78.084%
2. Oxygen	20.94%
3. Argon	0.93%
4. Carbon Dioxide	0.031%
5. Hydrogen	0.00005%s

Famous Waterfalls of India

Waterfall	Location	Height (m)
Jog or Garsopa	Sharavati river	255
Yena	Narmada river	183
Shiva Samudram	Kaveri river	90
Gokak	Ghatprabha river	55
Kakolat	Kakolat river	160
Dhuandhar	Narmada river	10
Hundru	Swarn Rekha river	74

India's Bordering Countries

Country	Border (KM)	Country	Border (KM)
Bangladesh	4096	Myanmar	1458
China	3917	Bhutan	587
Pakistan	3310	Afghanistan	80
Nepal	1752		

Bordering States of India

Country	Indian States on the Border
Pakistan	Gujrat, Rajasthan, Punjab, Jammu and Kashmir
Afghanistan	Jammu and Kashmir
China	Jammu and Kashmir, Himachal Pradesh, Uttrakhand, Sikkim, Arunachal Pradesh
Nepal	Uttar Pradesh, Bihar, West Bengal, Sikkim, Uttrakhand
Bhutan	Sikkim, West Bengal, Assam, Arunachal Pradesh
Bangladesh	West Bengal, Assam, Meghalaya, Tripura, Mizoram
Myanmar	Arunachal Pradesh, Nagaland, Manipur, Mizoram

Important Rivers of India

River	Place of Source	Merging Point/ Influx	Length (KM)
Ganges	Devprayag, the merging place of Alaknanda and Bhagirathi	The Bay of Bengal	2525
Brahma-putra	Chemayung-dung Glacier near Mansarovar Lake	The Bay of Bengal	2900
Sutlej	Rakastal near Mansarovar Lake	Chenab river	1050
Ravi	Rohtang Pass in Kangra district, Himachal Pradesh	Chenab river	720
Beas	Rohtang Pass	Sutlej river	470
Jhelum	Sheshnag Lake at Berenag (Jammu and Kashmir)	Indus river	1800
Yamuna	The western side of Bandar-poonchh (Yamunotri glacier)	Ganges river at Devprayag	1375
Chambal	Janapav hill near Mahu in Madhya Pradesh	Yamuna river	1050
Ghaghara	Matsatung glacier	Ganges river	1080
Gandak	Nepal	Ganges river	425
Kosi	North of Gosai Than Chot	Ganges river	730
Betwa	Vindhyachal mountains	Yamuna river	480
Son	The hills of Amarkantak	Ganges river	780
Krishna	Western Ghats hills near Mahabaleshvar	Bay of Bengal	1327
Godavari	The hill of Triyambak village, 64 K.M south-west to Nasik (Maharashtra)	Bay of Bengal	1465
Kaveri	Brahmagiri hills, Kurg district of Karnataka	Bay of Bengal	805
Tung-bhadra	Western Ghats in Karnataka	Krishna river	640
Pennar	Nandi Durg hills, Karnataka	Bay of Bengal	570
Mahanadi	Near Sinhawa in Rampur district of Madhya Pradesh	Bay of Bengal (Cuttuck)	858
Narmada	Amarkantak in the vindhya mountain range	Bay of Khambat	1057
Tapti	Near Multai city in Baitul district of Madhya Pradesh	Bay of Khambat	724
Mahi	Vindhya mountain range	Bay of Khambat	560
Luni	Nag Pahad (Aravali mountain range) near Ajmer district	Bay of Kutch	450
Ghagghar	Himalayas, near Kalka	Hanuman-gadh, Rajasthan	494
Sabarmati	The south-western part of Udaipur district, Aravali hills	The Rann of Kutch	416

Important Mountain Passes of India

Mountain Pass	Location
Karakoram, Zoji La, Banihal, Burzil	Jammu and Kashmir
Shipki La, Baralacha La	Himachal Pradesh
Mana, Lipulekh	Uttrakhand
Nathu La, Jelep La	Sikkim
Bomdi La, Difu	Arunachal Pradesh
Thal Ghat, Bhor Ghat	Maharashtra
Pal Ghat	Kerala

Important Cities Located on the Banks of the Rivers

City	River	City	River
Ahmedabad	Sabarmati	Nasik	Godavari
Kolkata	Hugli	Ujjain	Kshipra
Gauhati	Brahma-putra	Sri Nagar	Jhelum
Jabalpur	Narmada	Tiruchira-palli	Cauvery
Madurai	Vaigai	Dibrugadh	Brahma-putra
Panaji	Mandvi	Kota	Chambal
Pune	Mutha	Badrinath	Alaknanda
Surat	Tapti/Tapi	Lucknow	Gomati
Ayodhya	Saryu	Sri Rangpattnam	Cauvery
Pandharpur	Bhima	Ajmer	Luni
Hyderabad	Musi		

Important Lakes of India

Lake	State	Lake	State
Dal	Jammu and Kashmir	Pulicat	Tamilnadu
Wular	Jammu and Kashmir	Loktak	Manipur
Bairinag	Jammu and Kashmir	Sheshnag	Jammu and Kashmir
Rajsamand	Rajasthan	Anantnag	Jammu and Kashmir
Pichola	Rajasthan	Jai Samand	Rajasthan
Sambhar	Rajasthan	Didwana	Rajasthan
Sat Taal	Uttrakhand	Devatal	Uttrakhand
Nainital	Uttrakhand	Kolleru	Andhra Pradesh
Rakastal	Uttrakhand	Chilka	Odisha
Malatal	Uttrakhand	Lonar	Maharashtra
Hussain Sagar	Telangana	Bembanad	Kerala

Important River Valley Projects of India

Multi-Purpose Project	State	River
Bhima	Maharashtra	Pabna and Krishna
Hirakund Hydro-electric Project	Odisha	Mahanadi (this project has the world's biggest dam, 4801 meters)
Sardar Sarovar Project	M. P., Maharashtra, Rajasthan, Gujrat	Narmada (it's pond is named Indira Sagar, this is India's biggest man-made lake)
Narmada Sagar	Madhya Pradesh	Narmada
Chukha Hydro-electric Project	India, Bhutan	Wang Chhu
Indira Gandhi Canal	Rajasthan, Punjab, Haryana	Ravi, Beas, Sutlej
Farakka Barrage	West Bengal	Ganges (this project also works on cleaning debris from Kolkata port and desalination of Hugli river)
Damodar Valley Project	West Bengal and Jharkhand	Damodar river (this project is based on Tennessee Valley Project of USA)
Idukki	Kerala	Periyar river
Thien Dam	Punjab	Ravi river
Bhakhra Nangal Dam	Haryana, Himachal Pradesh, Rajasthan	Sutlej river (world's second highest dam, its pond is name Govind Sagar Lake)
Tulbul	Jammu and Kashmir	Jhelum river
Tanakpur Dam	India, Nepal	Mahakali river (India)
Salal Hydro-electricity	Jammu and Kashmir	Chenab
Pochampad	Telangana	Godavari
Kosi	Bihar	Kosi
Son Project	Bihar	Son
Kakrapar	Gujrat (Surat)	Tapti
Ukai (Uki)	Gujrat	Tapti
Mahi Project	Gujrat	Mahi
Sabarmati	Gujrat	Sabarmati
Gandhi Sagar	Madhya Pradesh	Chambal
Rana Pratap Sagar	Rajasthan	Chambal
Jawahar Sagar	Rajasthan	Chambal

Rihand Project	Uttar Pradesh	Rihand (a tributary of Son river, its pond is named Govind Vallabh Pant Sagar)
Sharda Project	Uttar Pradesh	Ghaghra-Sharda
Mata Tila Dam	Uttar Pradesh	Betwa
Tehri Dam	Uttrakhand	Bhagirathi
Nagarjuna Sagar	Andhra Pradesh/ Telangana	Krishna
Tunga-bhadra	Andhra Pradesh, Karnataka, Telangana	Tungabhadra
Nizam Sagar	Telangana	Tungabhadra
Shiva-samudram	Karnataka	Cauvery (the oldest hydroelectric project of India)

Main Climatic Regions of India

Climate	Related Region
Short-term Arid Climate	Malabar Coast, Konkan Coast, Andaman and Nicobar Islands
Tropical Savanah	The entire southern peninsula except Malabar and Coromandel coast
Arid Monsoon Climate	Eastern Tamilnadu, south-eastern region of Andhra Pradesh
Semi-arid Steppe	Middle Rajasthan, western Punjab, Haryana
Tropical Desert	Western part of Rajasthan, northern Gujrat, southern Haryana
Arid Cold Monsoon Climate	Northern India, Assam
Tundra Cliamte	Kashmir, Laddakh, northern Himachal Pradesh
Polar Climate	On the Himalayas above 5000 meters

Soil-Crop Distribution in India

Soil	Crop
Black soil	Cotton, sugarcane, tobacco, oilseeds
Alluvial soil	Rice, wheat, pulse, vegetables
Laterite soil	Coffee, rubber, pistachio, tapioca, ragi
Red-yellow soil	Rice, ragi, tobacco, groundnut
Desert soil	Maize, millet, gram, jute

National Parkal and Sanctuaries of India

Nation Park/ Sanctuary	Location
Kajiranga National Park (famous for one-horn rhinoceros)	Jorhat (Assam)
Manas Wildlife Sanctuary	Barpet (Assam)
Namdafa	Tirap (Arunachal Pradesh)
Pakkui Wildlife Sanctuary	Kameng (Arunachal Pradesh)
Chandraprabha Sanctuary	Varanasi (Uttar Pradesh)
Dudhwa National Park	Lakhimpur Khiri (Uttar Pradesh)
Jim Corbett National Park	Nainital (Uttrakhand)
Malan Animal Sanctuary	Paudi Gadhwal (Uttrakhand)
Govind Animal Sanctuary	Uttarkashi (Uttrakhand)
Similipal	Mayurganj, (Odisha)
Vedantgal Bird Sanctuary	Chingalpet, (Tamilnadu)
Bandipur National Park	Bandipur, (Karnataka)
Sharavati Valley	Shimoga, (Karnataka)
Rangathittu Bird Sanctuary	Mysore, (Karnataka)
Bhadra Sanctuary	Chikmangluru (Karnataka)
Nagahol National Park	Durg (Karnataka)
Someshvar	Kanara (Karnataka)
Tungbhadra	Bellary (Karnataka)
Periyar (famous for elephants)	Idukki (Kerala)
Gir National Park (famous for Indian lion)	Junagadh (Gujrat)
Dachigram Sanctuary	Srinagar (Jammu and Kashmir)
Jaldapara	Jalpaigudi (West Bengal)
Sundarban Tiger Reserve	Choubis Pargana (West Bengal)
Bhimbandh Sanctuary	Munger (Bihar)
Gautam Buddha	Gaya (Bihar)
Rajgir Sanctuary	Rajgir (Bihar)
Topchanchi Sanctuary	Dhanbad (Jharkhand)
Lavalong Sanctuary	Hazari Bagh (Jharkhand)
Dalma	Sinhbhum (Jharkhand)
Betwa Wildlife Sanctuary	Daltonganj (Jharkhand)
Panchmadhi (Manav National Park)	Hoshangabad (Madhya Pradesh)
Bori Sanctuary	Hoshangabad (Madhya Pradesh)
Kanha-Kisli National Park	Balaghat (Madhya Pradesh)

Gandhisagar	Mandsour (M. P.)
Bandhavgadh National Park	Shahdol (M. P.)
Fasil National Park	Mandla (Madhya Pradesh)
Panna National Park	Panna (Madhya Pradesh)
Satpuda National Park	Hoshangabad (M. P.)
Indravati National Park	Bastar (Chhatisgadh)
Badalkhol	Raigadh (Chhatisgadh)
Udyanti	Raipur (Chhatisgadh)
Sitanati	Raipur (Chhatisgadh)
Tamoi Pingla	Sarguja (Chhatisgadh)
Sanjay National Park	Sarguja (Chhatigadh)
Borivali Ntional Park	Mumbai (Maharashtra)
Pench National Park	Nagpur (Maharashtra)
Ranthambore Tiger Project	Savai Madhopur (Rajasthan)
Sariska	Alwar (Rajasthan)
Kevladev Ghana Bird Sanctuary	Bharatpur (Rajasthan)
Rohla National Park	Kullu (Himachal Pradesh)
Ross Island National Park	Ross Island (Andaman and Nicobar Islands)

Indian Flora

Flora	Region	Main Trees
Tropical Evergreen Forest	Western Ghats, Andaman and Nicobar Islands, North-East India	Rosewood, Mahogany, Ebony, Rubber
Tropical Deciduous Forest	Eastern Madhya Pradesh, northern Chhatisgadh, Jharkhand, Odisha	Teak, Rosewood, Mahua, Anwla, Sal, Semal, Silk-cotton
Tropical Arid Forest	Maharashtra, Karnataka, Tamilnadu, AP, werstern UP, Haryana, Punjab	Babul, Ber, Date, Neem, Khair, Palash
Desert Forest	Rajasthan, western Punjab, south-western Haryana	Babul, Kikar, Shrubs, Cactus
Mountain Forest	Above 1000 meters	A variety of fauna is found on that height

Irrigation in India: (respectively)

1. Wells
2. Canal
3. Other Sources
4. Tank

Most Irrigated States: (respectively)

1. Uttar Pradesh
2. Madhya Pradesh
3. Rajsthan
4. Gujarat

Soil in India

Soil	Region
Alluvial soil	The Ganges plain, Ahom valley, Gujrat, western coastal plain
Black soil	Vidarbha, western Madhya Pradesh, northern Karnataka, Tamilnadu, Bundelkhand
Red-Yellow soil	Madhya Pradesh, southern Uttar Pradesh, Nagpur plateau, Meghalaya plateau
Laterite soil	Tamilnadu, Kerala, Karnataka, Odisha, hilly regions os Assam
Piedmont soil	Northern Bihar, Odisha, Tamilnadu
Desert soil	Western Rajasthan, northern Gujrat, southern Haryana

Major Crop Producing States of India

Crop	States (in Descending Order)
Rice	West Bengal, Andhra Pradesh, U.P.
Wheat	Uttar Pradesh, Punjab, Haryana
Oilseeds	Rajasthan, Uttar Pradesh, Maharashtra
Corn	Andhra Pradesh, Karnataka, Rajasthan
Cereal	U.P., Punjab, Andhra Pradesh
Mustard	Rajasthan, U.P., Haryana
Sugarcane	U.P., Maharashtra, Tamilnadu
Cotton	Gujrat, Maharashtra, Andhra Pradesh
Pulse	Maharashtra, Madhya Pradesh, Andhra Pradesh

Tribes of India

Tribes	State	Tribe	State
Baiga, Bhuiya, Muriya	Madhya Pradesh	Khas	Uttrakhand
Bakkarwal	Jammu and Kashmir	Kook	Manipur, Assam
Bhotiya	Himayalan lowlands (Uttrakhand, Sikkim)	Kota	Tamilnadu
Chenchu	Andhra Pradesh	Lepcha	Sikkim
Angami, Eo	Nagaland	Mikir	Assam
Aptani	Arunachal Pradesh	Toda	Nilgiri hills
Badga	Himachal Pradesh	Mopla	Kerala
Irula	Tamilnadu	Munda	Jharkhand, West Bengal
Jarwa	Andaman and Nicobar Islands	Gond	M.P., Jharkhand, Chhatisgadh

Mineral Resources of India

Mineral	Place of Extraction
Aluminum	Madhya Pradesh, West Bengal, Maharashtra
Bauxite	Jharkhand, Bihar, Odisha, Andhra Pradesh
Chromite	Karnataka, Maharashtra, Jharkhand
Coal	West Bengal (Raniganj), Jharkhand (Jhariya, Bokaro, Karnpura), Maharashtra, Odisha, M.P.
Cobalt	Rajasthan, Kerala
Copper	Jharkhand, Rajasthan, Sikkim, Karnataka
Diamond	Madhya Pradesh (Panna), Uttar Pradesh (Banda)
Gold	Karnataka (Kolar, Hutti)
Iron Ore	Jharkhand, Odisha, Goa, Karnataka
Manganese	Maharashtra, Goa, Madhya Pradesh
Mica	Jharkhand, Tamilnadu
Tin	Jharkhand (Hazari Bagh)
Thorium	Kerala

Major National Highways

National Highway	From Where to Where	Total Distance (KM)
National Highway 1	Delhi-Pakistan Border	1226
National Highway 2	Delhi-Kolkata	1490
National Highway 3	Agra-Mumbai	1161
National Highway 4	Mumbai-Chennai	1415
National Highway 5	Kolkata-Chennai	1610
National Highway 6	Kolkata-Mumbai	1945
National Highway 7	Varanasi-Kanyakumari	2369
National Highway 8	Delhi-Jaipur-Mumbai	2058

Major Aluminum Companies of India

Company	Contributing Country	Major Centers
BALCO	Soviet Union	Korba and Koyna
NALCO	France	Damanjodi (Odisha)
HINDALCO	USA	Renukut (U.P.)
INDALCO	Canada	J. K. Nagar, Muri, Alwai
MALCO	Italy	Chennai, Mettur, Selam

Indian Railway Zones and their Headquarters

Zone	Headquarter
Middle Railway	Mumbai V. T
Eastern Railway	Kolkata
Northern Railway	New Delhi
North-East Railway	Gorakhpur
North-East Border Railway	Maligaon, Gauhati
Southern Railway	Chennai
South-Middle Railway	Secunderabad
South-Eastern Railway	Kolkata
Western Railway	Mumbai, Church Gate
Eastern-Middle Railway	Hazipur
North-Western Railway	Jaipur
Eastern Coastal Railway	Bhubaneswar
North-Middle Railway	Allahabad
South-East-Middle Railway	Bilaspur
South-Western Railway	Hubli
Western-Middle Railway	Jabalpur
Kolkata Metro	Kolkata

Geographical Pseudonyms of Indian Cities/States

Pseudonym	Official Name
Manchester of India	Ahmedabad
The Curse of Bihar	Kosi river
The Heart of Rajasthan	Ajmer
The Land of the Five Rivers	Punjab
The Hollywood of India	Mumbai
The Glory of Rajasthan	Chittidgadh
Blue Mountains	Nilgiri Hills
Steel City	Jamshedpur
The Bowl of Rice	Chhatisgadh
The Curse of Bengal	Damodar river
The Queen of the Hills	Mussoorie
The Fruit Basket	Himachal Pradesh
The Gateway of India	Mumbai
The Son of the Sea	Lakshadweep
The Jewel of Karnataka	Mysore
The Garden of India	Bengaluru
The Kashmir of South	Kerala
The City of the Festivals	Madurai
India's Spice Garden	Kerala

Major International Airports of India	
Name	**Location**
Chhatrapati Shivaji International Airport (Santacruz)	Mumbai
Subhash Chandra Bose Airport (Damdam)	Kolkata
Indira Gandhi International Airport	Delhi
Mmenambakam International Airport	Chennai
Tiruannantpuram International Airport	Tiruannantpuram
Amritsar International Airport	Amritsar
Beghampet International Airport	Hyderabad
Kochchi International Airport	Kochchi
Lokpriya Gopinath Bordoliyo International Airport	Gauhati
Goa International Airport	Goa
Bengaluru International Airport	Bengaluru
Sardar Vallabhbhai Patel International Airport	Ahmedabad

Types of Railway Lines	
Type	**Distance Between the Rails (m)**
Broad Gaze	1.676
Meter Gaze	1.00s
Narrow Gaze	0.7610

National Waterways			
Waterway	**Distance (KM)**	**Expansion**	**River**
NW-1	1620	Allahabad to Haldia	Ganges
NW-2	891	Sadiya to Dhubri Patti	Brahmaputra
NW-3	205	Kollam to Kottapuram	Champakkara
NW-4	1905	Kakinada to Marakkaanam	Krishna-Godavari
NW-5	623	Tal-cher-Dhamra	Brahmani River
NW-6	121	Lakhipur to Bhanga	Barak

Shifting Agriculture in India	
Shifting Agriculture	**State**
Pondu	Andhra Pradesh
Kumari	Western Kerala
Kamaan, Vinga, Dhavi	Odisha
Bantra	South-eastern Rajasthan
Jara, Erka	South India
Jhum	North-east India
Veshar, Dahivar, Dipa	Madhya Pradesh

Major Ports of India	
Western Coast	**Eastern Coast**
Kandla (Free Trade Zone established)	Paradip (iron export to Japan)
Mumbai (the biggest and the busiest)	Vishakapattnam (the deepest port)
Jawaharlal Nehru (ultra-modern)	Ennore (modern port of private sector)
Marmugaon	Tutikorin (the southernmost port)
Manglore (Kudremukh iron ore export)	Port Blair (geographically important)
Kochin (natural port)	

Industrial Boards of India	
Industrial Board	**Year**
Cottage Industry Board	1948
Central Silk Board	1949
All India Handloom Board	1950
All India Khadi and rural Industry Board	1954
All India Handicraft Board	1953
Small Industry Board	1954
Central Selling Organization (Chennai)	1958

Different Types of Agriculture	
Sericulture	Silkworm agriculture
Apiculture	Honeybee agriculture
Pisciculture	Fish agriculture
Floriculture	Flower agriculture
Viticulture	Grapes agriculture
Vermiculture	Earthworm agriculture
Pomoculture	Fruit agriculture
Olericulture	Vegetable agriculture
Horticulture	Gardening
Aeroportic	To grow plants in air
Hydroportic	To grow plants in water

Production Related revolutions of India	
Green Revolution	Food-grains production
White Revolution	Milk production
Blue Revolution	Fishery production
Brown Revolution	Fertilizer production
Silver Revolution	Egg production
Yellow Revolution	Oilseed production
Black Revolution	Biodiesel production

Red Revolution	Tomato/Meat production
Pink Revolution	Jhinga fish production
Brownish/Badami Revolution	Spices production

Major Seas Around the World

Sea	Area (square KM)	Depth (Meters)
South China Sea	81,42,960	1,200
Caribbean Sea	27,53,000	2,400
Mediterranean Sea	25,03,000	1,485
Bering Sea	22,68,180	1,400
East China Sea	12,49,150	188
Andaman Sea	7,97,720	865
Okhotsk Sea	15,27,570	840

Major Trenches Around the World

Trench	Depth (mtr)	Location
Challenger/Mariana Trench	11,022	Pacific Ocean
Tonga Trench	9,000	Pacific Ocean
Mindanao Trench	10,500	Pacific Ocean
Puerto Rico Trench	8,392	Atlantic Ocean
Romanche Trench	7,254	Atlantic Ocean
Sunda Trench	8,152	Indian Ocean

Mountains of the World

Mountain	Location	Highest Peak	Height (Mtr)
Himalaya	Asia	Mount Everest	8848
Andes	South America	Aconcagua	6960
Rockies	North America	Mount Albert	4400
Karakoram	Asia	Godwin Austin/K2	8611
Great Dividing Range	Australia	Mount Kosciuszko	2228
Ural	Russia	Narodnaya	1894
Atlas	Africa	Toubkal	4165
Alps	Europe	Mount Black	4807
Alaska Range	Alaska	Mount Denali/ McKinley	6194
Caucasus Range	Europe	Elbrus	5633

Continents of the World

Continent	Area (%)	Continent	Area (%)
Asia	29.5	Antarctica	9.6
Africa	20.0	Europe	6.5
North America	16.3	Australia	5.2
South America	11.8		

Major Rivers of the World

River	Place of Origin	Oustfall	Length (KM)
Nile	Victoria Lake	Medite-rranean Sea	6650
Amazon	Andes mountains (Peru)	Atlantic ocean	6428
Yangtze Kiang	Tibetan Plateau	China sea	6300
Mississippi-Missouri	Itasca lake (USA)	Bay of Mexico	6275
Yenisei	Mount Tanuola	Arctic sea	5539
Hwang Ho	Mount Kunlun	Bay of China	5464
Ob	Mount Altai, Russia	Bay of Ob	5410
Congo	The merger of Lualia and Lapula rivers	Atlantic ocean	4700
Lina	Mount Baikal	Laptev sea	4400
Mekong	Tibetan Plateau	South China sea	4350

Major Volcanos of the World

Volcano	Country/Location
Cotopaxi	Ecuador
Popocatepetl	Mexico
Mauna Loa	America (Hawaii Islands)
Erebus	Antarctica
Etna	Italy (Sicily)
Saint Helens	America
Vesuvius	Italy (Bay of Naples)
Kilauea	Hawaii Islands
Stromboli	Iceland (Mediterranean sea)
Krakatoa	Indonesia

Islands of the World		
Island	**Area (square KM)**	**Location**
Greenland	27,75,000	Arctic ocean
New Guinea	7,89,000	West Pacific ocean
Borneo	7,51,0000	Indian ocean
Madagascar	5,87,041	Indian ocean
Baffin Island	5,07,451	North Pole Ocean
Sumatra	4,22,200	Indian ocean
Honshu	2,30,092	North Pacific ocean

World's Major Geographical Discoveries	
Discoverer	**Discovery**
R. Amundsen (Norway)	First person to reach South Pole (1911 A. D)
Robert Pierre (USA)	The discovery of North Pole (1909 A. D)
Christopher Columbus	Western Islands (1492 A. D), South America (1498 A. D)
Captain Cook	Hawaii Islands (1770 A.D)
Copernicus (Poland)	The Solar System (1540 A. D)
Ferdinand de Lesseps	The builder of Suez Canal (1869 A. D)
Kepler	The rotation speed of planets (1600 A. D)
Magllan	Traveled across world, the discovery of Pacific ocean from south of Atlantic (1519 A. D)
Vasco da Gama (Portugal)	Came to India via Cape of Good Hope (1498 A. D)

Famous Nicknames of Countries/Places	
Nickname	**Country/Place**
Land of the Elephants	Laos
The Land of the Midnight	Norway
The Land of Pagoda	Myanmar(Burma)
Land of the Lakes	Finland
The Sugar Bowl	Cuba
The Heart of Europe	Switzerland
The City of Rivers	Venice
The Key to Mediterranean	Gibraltar
The Black Continent	Africa
The Pearl of the East	Singapore
The Land of the Sunrise	Japan
The Holy Land	Yerushalem
The Land of the Kangaroos	Australia
Island of Pearls	Bahrain
The City of the Golden Gate	San Francisco
The Britain of South	New Zealand
The Heaven of Europe	Switzerland
The Roof of the World	Pamir Plateau
The City of Seven Hills	Rome
The Land of the Pyramids	Egypt
The Forbidden City	Lhasa (Tibet)

Major Lakes Around the World			
Lake	**Area (square KM)**	**Maximum Depth (Meters)**	**Location/ Country**
Caspian Sea	3,71,000	980	Eastern European countries and Iran
Superior Lake	82,350	406	Canada and USA
Victoria (Nyasa)	69,500	80	Uganda, Tanzania and Kenya
Aral Sea	65,000	68	Russia
Huron Lake	59,600	228	Canada, USA
Michigan Lake	58,000	281	USA
Tanganyka Lake	32,900	1435	Congo, Tanzania, Zambia and Zaire
Great Barrier Lake	31,800	82	Canada
Baikal	30,500	1940	Russia
Malawi (Nyasa) Lake	29,600	678	Mozambique

World's Major Deserts		
Desert	**Area (square KM)**	**Country**
Sahara	84,00,000	Algeria, Chad, Libya, Mali, Mauritania, Niger, Sudan, Tunisia, Egypt, Morocco
Australia	15,50,000	Australia
Arab	13,00,000	Saudi Arabia, Yemen, Syria
Gobi	10,40,000	Magnolia, China
Kalahari	5,20,000	Botswana
Taklamakan	3,20,000	Xinjiang (China)
Namib	3,10,000	Namibia
Karakum	2,70,000	Turkmenistan
Thar	2,60,000	India, Pakistan
Atacama	1,80,000	Northern Chile

Some Major Cities Situated on the Banks of Rivers	
City	**River**
London (England)	Thames
Berlin (Germany)	Spree
Mosco (Russia)	Moskva
Vienna (Austria)	Danube
Lisbon (Portugal)	Tagus
Leningrad (Russia)	Neva
Budapest (Hungary)	Danube
Belgrade (Yugoslavia)	Danube
Warsaw (Poland)	Vistula
Rome (Italy)	Tiber
Paris (France)	Seine
Stalingrad (Russia)	Volga
Madrid (Spain)	Manzanares
Baghdad (Iraq)	Tigris
Khartoum (Sudan)	Nile
Ankara (Turkey)	Kizil
Quebec (Canada)	Saint Lawrence
Cairo (Egypt)	Nile
Perth (Australia)	Swan
Tokyo (Japan)	Arakawa
Ottawa (Canada)	Saint Lawrence
Sidney (Australia)	Darling
Montreal (Canada)	Saint Lawrence
New York (USA)	Hudson
Washington D. C (USA)	Potomac
Karachi (Pakistan)	Indus
Lahore (Pakistan)	Ravi
Kabul (Afghanistan)	Kabul
Shanghai (China)	Yangtze Kiang
Chatgaon (Bangladesh)	Karnaphuli
Buenos Aires (Argentina)	La Plata

Major Canals around the World		
Canal	**Length (KM)**	**Merger Point**
Suez Canal	169	Mediterranean Sea and Red Sea
Panama Canal	58	Atlantic and Pacific Oceans
Keel Canal	98	Northern and Baltic Sea
Erie Canal	584	Erie Lake and Michigan Lake
Soo Canal	—	Superior Lake and Huron Lake

Grassland of the World			
Steppe	**Country**	**Steppe**	**Country**
Pampas	Argentina	Downs	Australia
Prairie	America	Canterbury	New Zealand
veld	South America	Steppe	Eurasia

Shifting Agriculture around the World	
Agriculture	**Country**
Chenna	Sri Lanka
Huma	Java
Kaigin	Philippines
Lahang	Indonesia and Malesia
Roka	Brazil
Tamarai	Thailand
Konuko	Venezuela

Major Waterfalls around the World		
Waterfall	**Country**	**Height (Feet)**
Angel	Venezuela	2,648
Cuquenan	Venezuela	2,000
Ribbon	USA	1,612
Upper Yosemite	USA	1,430
Tugela	South America	1,350

Changed Names of Famous Cities/Locations			
Old Name	**New Name**	**Old Name**	**New Name**
Abyssinia	Ethiopia	Persia	Iran
Campuchsia	Cambodia	Burma	Myanmar
British Guana	Guana	Nippon	Japan
Formosa	Taiwan	Malaya	Malaysia
Northern Rhodesia	Zambia	Ceylon	Sri Lanka
South Western Africa	Namibia	Sandwich Island	Hawaii Island
Zaire	Congo	Salisbury	Harare
Dutch East Indies	Indonesia	Siam	Thailand
Gold Coast	Ghana	Holland	Netherland
Peking	Beijing	Suvarn Deep	Java
Saint Petersburg	Leningrad	Meso-potamia	Iraq

Silk Research Institutes of India	
Institute	**Locations**
Central Silk Research Institute	Mysore and Brahmaputra
Central Eri Silk Research Institute	Mendipathar, Meghalaya
Central Tasar Research institute	Ranchi, Jharkhand

Borders of Countries	
Durand Line	Pakistan and Afghanistan
Hindenburg Line	Germany and Poland
49th Parallel Line	USA and Canada
McMahon Line	India and Tibet/China
Maginot Line	France and Germany
38th Parallel Line	North and South Korea
Odder-Nisi Line	Germany and Poland
Red cliff Line	India and Pakistan

- Which authority in India is reported responsible for the set up the refineries Mathura, Digboi and Panipat- **Indian Oil Corporation Ltd.**
- Who is known as "Father of white Revolution" in India- **V. Kurien**
- The Radcliffe line is boundary between- **India and Pakistan**
- Identify the Gulf that has a potential for harnessing of tidal energy in India- **Gulf of Cambay**
- The state having largest area of forest cover in India is -**Madhya Pradesh**
- Which year is called a Great Divide in the demographic history in India-**1921**
- Which is the only state in India that produces saffron- **Jammu And Kashmir**
- Which food grain crop is occupied the largest part of the cropped area in India- **Rice**
- The number of major languages, recognized in the Indian Union as official language, are- **22**
- Which state in India has the largest number of district- **Uttar Pradesh**
- The oldest rocks in India are reported from- **Dharwar region, Karnataka**
- Duduma falls are located on which of the following rivers in India- **Machkund River**
- Ninai falls are located on the watercourse of which of the following rivers-**Narmada**
- Which of the waterfalls are located on Bihad river, a tributary of Tons river- **Chachai falls**
- Abbey falls are located in the geographical proximity of:-**Western Ghats**
- Which of the waterfalls is located on the the Leh-Manali highway in Himachal Pradesh- **Rehala falls**
- Which of the waterfalls is located on the Aghanashini River in Karnataka- **Unchalli falls**
- Buhraghagh falls/Lodh falls are located on which of the following rivers in India:- **Burha River**
- Katki waterfalls are located in which of the following States- **Andhra Pradesh**
- Talakona, the highest waterfall in Andhra Pradesh is situated in which of the following districts- **Chittor**
- Chitrakoot falls are located in which of the following States- **Chattisgarh**
- The river Narmada is originate from..... **Amarkantak**
- Which one of the following lakes is a salt water lake-**Sambhar**
- Which one of the following is the longest river of the Peninsular India- **Godavari**
- A landmass bounded by sea on three sides is referred to as-**Peninsula**

INDIAN POLITY

Indian Polity

- The Constituent Assembly was created – **on the recommendation of Cabinet Mission (1946)**
- How long did it take to prepare the India constitution – **2 years, 11 months and 18 days**
- When was a separate Constituent Assembly for Pakistan was created – **on 26th July, 1947**
- The number of members in the Constituent Assembly at the beginning – **389**
- How many members did remain in the Constituent Assembly after the partition – **299**
- How many Princely States were in India at the time of the Independence – **542**
- The nature of India constitution is – **unitary and federal**

Various Committees of the Constituent Assembly and Their Heads

Committee on the Rules of Procedure	Dr. Rajendra Prasad
Union Constitution Committee	Jawaharlal Nehru
States Committee	Jawaharlal Nehru
Drafts Committee	Dr. Bhimrao Ambedkar
Union Powers Committee	Jawaharlal Nehru

- The Princely State that did not participate in the Constituent Assembly – **Hyderabad**
- The temporary chairman of the first meeting of the Constituent Assembly (9th December, 1946) – **Doctor Sachichidanand Sinha**
- Doctor Rajendra Prasad was elected the chairman of Constituent Assembly on – **11th December, 1946**
- The Constitutional Advisor of the Constituent Assembly – **V. N. Rao**
- The chairman of the Drafts Committee (established on 29th August, 1947) – **Doctor B. R. Ambedkar**
- The first Law Minister of India – **Doctor B. R. Ambedkar**
- The chairman of the Flag Committee – **J. B. Kriplani**
- To what did Doctor Ambedkar refer as the ' soul of the constitution' – **The right to Constitutional Remedies**

Various Committees of the Constituent Assembly and Their Heads

Country	Source
Britain	Parliamentary rule, law making process, single nationality
USA	Fundamental rights, judicial review, autonomy of the judiciary, the establishment of Supreme Court and judicial powers, impeachment of the President
Canada	Federal system, vesting the Residuary Powers with the Center
Ireland	Directive Principles
Germany	Emergency Provisions
Australia	The language of the Preamble, Concurrent List, Center-State Relations
Japan	Procedures established by law
France	Democracy
Russia	Fundamental Duties

- 'The Key to the Constitution' – **The Preamble**
- The terms 'secular' and 'socialist' were added into the preamble by – **42nd Amendment**
- The draft of the constitution was debated upon for – **114 days**
- When was the Indian constitution accepted – **on 26th November, 1949**
- When was the constitution implemented – **on 26th January, 1950**
- The father of Indian Constitution – **Doctor B. R. Ambedkar**
- Who called the Indian constitution a 'semi-federal constitution' – **Wheeler**
- The number of Articles, Schedules and Parts in the first adopted draft of the constitution – **395, 8 and 22 respectively**
- The number of Articles at present – **more than 444**
- The number of Schedules at present – **12**
- How many languages were registered in the 8th Schedule – **22**
- The total number of states in India at present – **29**
- The number of states mentioned in the first draft of the constitution – **14**

Parts and Articles of the Constitution and their Description	
Part/Article	Description
Part-1/Articles 1-4	The Union and its Territory, creation of new states
Part-2/Articles 5-11	Citizenship
Part-3/Articles 12-35	Fundamental Rights
Part-4/Article 36-51	Directive Principles of the State
Part-4A/Article 51A	Fundamental Duties of the Citizens (added through the 42nd amendment in 1976)
Part-5/Articles 52-151	Related to the Union Government
Part-6/Articles 152-237	Related to state governments
Part-7/Article 238	It is related to Part B of the first Article, removed in 1956 via 7th amendment
Part-8/Articles 239-242	The administration of Union Territories
Part-9/Article 243, P-243 Z. G	Municipal Council
Part-18/Articles 352-360	Emergency Procedures
Part-19/Articles 361-367	Miscellaneous
Part-20/Article 368	Constitutional Amendments
Part-21/Articles 369-392	Temporary, Changeable and Special Laws
Part-22/Articles 393-395	Abbreviations, beginning, authorized Hindi version and Cancellation

- The name of the country used in the constitution – **Bharat or India**
- ♦ The largest part of the constitution – **5th**
- ♦ Which part of the constitution is dubbed as the "Magna Carta of India' – **3rd Part**
- ♦ The Federal Judiciary is mentioned in – **Chapter 4 of Part 5**
- ♦ What topics are dealt with in Part 15th and 18th – **Election and Emergency Procedures respectively**
- ♦ Which country first adopted a written constitution – **USA**
- ♦ The biggest written constitution – **Indian Constitution**
- ♦ The power to create new states are provided in the Article – **2**
- ♦ According to Article-3, who has the power to create new states, or to change, boundary or name of the states – **the Parliament**
- ♦ The first state to be created on linguistic basis – **Andhra Pradesh (in 1953)**
- ♦ The 7th Constitutional Amendment (1956) deals with – **restructuring of states on linguistic basis**
- ♦ Who was the chairman of States Restructuring Commission – **Fazal Ali**
- ♦ Goa was given the status of a full state by – **56th Amendment, 1987**
- ♦ When did Sikkim get the status of a full state (22nd state of India) – **by 36th Amendment, 1975**
- ♦ Delhi got the full status as the capital of India by – **69th Amendment, 1991**
- ♦ The sovereignty of the constitution is vested in – **the citizens of India**
- ♦ The model of Federal system (administrative model) is adopted from – **Canada**
- ♦ India parliamentary rule system and law-making process is influenced by – **Britain**
- ♦ The Fundamental Rights and Fundamental Duties have been adopted from the constitutions of – **USA and Russia respectively**
- ♦ The Directive Principles have been adopted from the constitution of – **Ireland**
- ♦ Where are the 'Directive Principles' mentioned in the constitution – **in Part-4, Articles 36-51**
- ♦ Emergency Procedures has been adopted from the constitution of – **Germany**
- ♦ Concurrent List has been adopted from the constitution of – **Australia**
- ♦ The procedure of Constitutional Amendments has been adopted from the constitution of – **South Africa**
- ♦ Which Article gives the Parliament the powers to amend the constitution – **Article 368, Part-20**
- ♦ The first amendment in the constitution was made in the year – **1951**
- ♦ At present, what is the number of issues mentioned in State, Union and Concurrent Lists – **62, 98 and 52 respectively**
- ♦ Who has the power to make laws on the issues mentioned in the Concurrent List – **both State and the Center**
- ♦ Forest and environment is mentioned in

– **Concurrent List**

- Law and order is mentioned in – **State List**
- Education and newspapers are mentioned in – **Concurrent List**
- Railway, postage and defense are mentioned in – **Union List**
- Panchayti Raj is mentioned in– **State List**
- 11th Schedule is related to–**Panchayti Raj**
- The smallest unit of Panchayti Raj is – **the village Panchayat**
- Who is responsible for conducting the village Panchayat elections – **State**
- Who represents the government at the Panchayat level – **The Gram Sevak**
- Panchayti Raj system (tri-level) was started on the recommendation of – **the report of Balwant Rai Mehta Committee**
- The Panchayti Raj system was first implemented at – **in Nagour, Rajasthan on 2nd October, 1959**
- The 73rd Constitutional Amendment deals with – **Panchayti Raj system**
- What is India's citizenship model – **Single citizenship**
- The minimum age for obtaining and losing Indian citizenship is – **10 years and 7 years respectively**
- Which part of the constitution deals with Fundamental Rights – **Part-3 (Articles 12-35)**
- How many Fundamental Rights were mentioned in the first draft of the constitution – **7**
- The number of Fundamental Rights in the constitution at present – **6**
- By which amendment was the Right to Property deleted from the Fundamental Rights and refined as a Legal Right (Schedule-300 A) – **44th Amendment, 1977**
- Who has the right to amend the Fundamental Rights – **the Parliament**
- The most important writ issued in defense of Individual Liberty – **Habeas Corpus**
- What is the number of Fundamental Duties mentioned in Article 51 A at present – **11**
- The Fundamental Rights were assembled in the constitution by – **42nd Amendment, 1976**
- Which committee recommended that the Fundamental Rights should be added into the Constitution – **Sardar Swarn Singh Committee**
- Which article deals with the abolition of untouchability – **Article 17**
- Anti-Untouchability Act was passed in the year – **1955**
- The Freedom of Press is mentioned in the Article – **19 (1) A**
- 'The Fourth Pillar' refers to – **The press**
- The Liberty of Life and Body is mentioned in – **Article 21**
- Which article protects the interests of the minorities – **Article 29**
- Which amendment ensures the free and compulsory education of the children from 6-14 years – **86th Amendment, 2002**
- Which article states that employing children below 14 years of age into dangerous labor is a crime – **Article 24**
- The parts of the Parliament are – **the President, Loksabha, Rajya Sabha**
- Who is the first citizen of India – **the President**
- Which article ensures the provision for presidential post – **Article 52**
- Who inaugurates each session of the parliament – **the President**
- India's first president – **Dr. Rajendra Prasad**
- To whom can the president offer his resignation – **the Vice-President**
- The tenure of the president and the vice-president is - **5 years**
- The only lawful process to dismiss the president from her post – **the Impeachment (Article 61)**
- What is the process for starting the Impeachment – **the President is informed about the impeachment against her 14 days prior to the start of the impeachment**
- The monthly salaries of the President and the Vice-President are – **1,50,000 and 1,25,000 Rupees respectively**
- The minimum age limit for the post of President, Vice-President and Governor is – **35 years**
- Who can dissolve the Parliament – **the President (Article 85)**
- Who can pardon the death penalty – **the President (Article 72)**
- The only Chief Justice who was elected the President as well – **M. Hidaytullah**
- Who participates in the election of the President – **the Parliament and the members of the state Legislative Assemblies**
- How many members can the President appoint in the Lok Sabha and the Rajya Sabha – **2 (Anglo-Indians) and 12 respectively**

- Who appoints the Prime Minister, Governors, Attorney General, the judges of the Supre and the High Courts and Chief Election Officer – **the President**
- Who appoints the Vice-Chairman of Planning Commission – **the Cabinet**
- The process for the election of the President – **Single Transferable Vote system**
- The President appoints the ministers with the consultation of – **the Prime Minister**
- Who announces the Presidential Rule (under Article 356) in a state – **the President**
- The person who was elected the President unopposed – **Neelam Sanjeev Reddy**
- The presidents that died during their office tenure – **Fakhruddin Ali Ahmed and Zakir Hussain**
- The first Acting President – **V. V. Giri**
- The first woman candidate to contest the election for the post of President – **Captain Lakshmi Sehgal**
- The first woman president of India – **Pratibha Patil**
- Who issues ordinances when both the houses are not in session – **the President**
- Who swears-in the President – **the Chief Justice of India**
- The President can call the Joint Session of the Parliament, who acts as its head – **the Speaker of the Lok Sabha**
- The decisions in the Joint Session of the Parliament are made on the basis of – **majority**
- The salary of the President and the Vice-President is paid through – **a consolidated fund**
- The first presidential rule (Article 356) was imposed – **in Punjab, 1951**
- The minimum and maximum limit of the Presidential Rule – **6 months and 3 years respectively**
- Which Article ordains that 'India shall have one Vice-President' – **Article 63**
- Who oversees the presidential duties while the presidential post remains vacant – **the Vice-President**
- The electoral disputes of the presidential and vice-presidential elections are heard by – **the Supreme Court**
- The first Vice-President – **Dr. S. Radhakrishnan**
- If the President and the Vice-President both are absent, who oversees the Presidential duties – **the Chief Justice of Supreme Court**
- The salaries of the President and the Vice President have been increased to- **Rs 5 lakh and Rs 4 lakh per month respectively**
- The ex-officio head of the Rajya Sabha – **the Vice-President**
- Who participates in the election of the Vice-President – **all members of the Parliament**
- Which Article ordains the post of the Prime Minister – **Article 74 (i)**
- The first Prime Minister – **Jawaharlal Nehru**
- The first Vice Prime Minister – **Sardar Vallabhbhai Patel**
- Who can form and dissolve the Cabinet – **the Prime Minister**
- Who can form and dissolve the Cabinet – **the Prime Minister**
- The first Prime Minister to be deposed from his post via the Motion of No-confidence – **Vishwanath Pratap Singh**
- The first non-Congress Prime Minister – **Morarji Desai**
- The first totally non-Congress Prime Minister – **Atal Bihari Vajpayee**
- When did Atal Bihari Vajpayee address the UNO for the first time – **in 1977**
- The Prime Minister who was a member of the any House at the time of swearing-in – **P. V. Narsimha Rao**
- The first Prime Minister to offer his resignation – **V. V. Giri**
- The Prime Minister who could not attend even one session of the Parliament–**Choudhary Charan Singh**
- The Rajya Sabha was formed on – **3rd April, 1952**
- The Lok Sabha was formed on – **6th May, 1952**
- The Legislature of the Union government – **Lok Sabha**
- The Lower House of the Parliament – **Lok Sabha**
- The Speaker of the Lok Sabha offers her resignation to – **the Deputy Speaker of the Lok Sabha**
- The permanent and the Upper House of the Parliament – **Rajya Sabha**
- The maximum member limit in the Lok Sabha and the Rajya Sabha is – **552 and 250 respectively**
- The tenure of the members of the Rajya Sabha – **6 years**

- The tenure of the members of the Lok Sabha – **5 years**
- How many members are there in the Estimate Committee – **30 (all from the Lok Sabha)**
- What is the minimum age requirement for becoming a member of the Lok Sabha and Rajya Sabha – **25 and 30 years respectively**
- The tenure of the Lok Sabha can be extended in case of – **an emergency**
- The leader of the opposition was acknowledged for the first time – **in 1969**
- The first leaders of opposition in the Lok Sabha and the Rajya Sabha – **Kamlapati Tripathi and Ramsubhag Singh respectively**
- The Union Cabinet is answerable for its conduct to – **Lok Sabha**
- The minimum number of attendance necessary to run the session of the Lok Sabha – **1/10th of the total members**
- The members of the Rajya Sabha are elected through the process of – **Single Transferable Vote system**
- The first Lok Sabha Speaker – **G. V. Malvankar**
- How many members of the Rajya Sabha get retired every second year – **One third**
- The first woman Secretary of the Rajya Sabha – **B. S. Ramadevi**
- Which states sends the maximum number of representatives in Lok Sabha and Rajya Sabha – **Uttar Pradesh**
- The Union Budget is presented at – **Lok Sabha**
- The Section 302 of IPC is related to – **murder**
- The Money Bill is defined in – **Article 110**
- The Financial Bill is defined in – **Article 112**
- Who decides whether the Financial Bill is Money Bill or not – **the Speaker of Lok Sabha**
- The Rajya Sabha can keep the Money Bill to itself for – **14 days maximum**
- Whose permission is required before presenting the Money Bill into the Lok Sabha – **the President**
- Who declares financial emergency under Article 360 – **the President**
- The Money Bill is presented at – **Lok Sabha**
- Which Article permits one person be appointed the Governor of two or more States – **Article 153 (2)**
- Who can question the legality of the action of the Governor – **the Legislative Assembly**
- Who is the chairman of the state executive – **the Governor**
- The lower house of the state legislature – **Vidhan Sabha**
- The upper house of the state legislature – **legislative Council (Vidhan Parishad)**
- The number of Anglo-Indians appointed by the Governor in the Vidhan Sabha – **1**
- The minimum and maximum number of member limit in the Vidhan Sabha – **60 and 500 respectively**
- The number of Legislative Council appointed by the Governor – **1/6th**
- The minimum age requirement for becoming the member of the Legislative Council and Vidhan Sabha – **30 and 25 respectively**
- The Ordinance issued by the Governor is accepted by – **the Legislative Assembly**
- Which Article ordains that the state should have Legislative Assembly – **under Article 170**
- Who is the head of state Cabinet – **the Chief Minister**
- United Nations was established on – **24th October, 1945**
- What is referred to as the 'Mini Constitution' – **the 42nd Amendment (1976)**
- For how long can a minister remain on her post without holding the position as the member of the Parliament–**6 months**
- National Security Act was passed in the year –**1980**
- The tenure for the members of UPSC and Chief Election Officer – **6 years**
- What is the maximum time limit for the Parliament to accept the declaration of emergency – **1 month**
- The duration of Question Hour – **1 hour**
- What is Zero Hour – **the time after the Question Hour**
- The time between 12 to 1 is known as – **Zero Hour**
- The 10th Schedule is related to – **Anti-Defection Act**
- Anti-Defection Act was validated by – **52nd Amendment (1952)**
- The first non-Congress government – **in Kerala (1957)**

- The tenure of the Parliamentary Committees – **1 year**
- The first person to resign from the Union Cabinet – **Shyama Prasad Mukherjee**
- Who prepared the blueprint of the Parliament House – **Sir Herbert Baker and Edwin Lutyens**
- The Parliament House was inaugurated – **on 18th January, 1927 by Lord Irwin**
- The Schedule Castes and the Schedule Tribes were provided reservation by – **8th Amendment (1959)**
- The only woman member of the Constitutional Review Commission – **Shrimati Sumitra G. Kulkarni**
- Prasar Bharti Act was passed – **on 15th September, 1997**
- Warren Hastings was appointed the Governor of Bengal by – **Regulating Act of 1773**
- The trade monopoly of the Company was abolished by – **the Charter Act of 1813**
- Lord William Bentinck was appointed the first Governor-General of India by – **Charter Act of 1833**
- Mandal Commission was formed in – **1979**
- The post of the Governor-General was renamed as Viceroy by – **Government of India Act, 1858**
- When was the Dual government was started in what year and when was it ended – **1921 and 1st April 1937 respectively**
- The state autonomy was implemented on – **1st April, 1938**
- The number of members in the restructured Constituent Assembly – **299**
- The meeting of the Inter-state Council is organized – **thrice every year**

Swearing-in and Resignation Protocols		
Post	Swearing-in	Resignation
President	Chief Justice	Vice President
Vice President	President	President
Governor	The Chief Justice of the State High Court	President
Chief Justice of India	President	President
Prime Minister	President	President

- The provision for joint session of the Parliament is mentioned in – **under Article 108**
- The first Official Language Commission was formed in – **1955**
- The chairman of the first Official Language Commission – **B. G. Khare**
- The provision for the establishment of Supreme Court is mentioned in – **Article 124**
- How many judges are appointed in the Supreme Court – **31 (1 Chief Justice and 30 judges)**
- The number of High Courts in India – **24**
- Who is deemed the protector and interpreter of the Constitution – **the Supreme Court**
- Who is the First Law Officer – **the Attorney-General of India**
- Who was the first Chief Justice of India – **Harilal Jekisundas Kaniya**
- How many judges (including the Chief Justice) were there in the Supreme Court in the beginning – **8**
- The Union Territory that is under the jurisdiction of the Punjab and Haryana High Court – **Chandigarh**
- The Union Territory that is under the jurisdiction of Calcutta High Court – **Andaman and Nicobar Islands**
- The Union Territory that is under the jurisdiction of Madras High Court – **Pondicherry**
- The Union Territory that is under the jurisdiction of Kerala High Court – **Lakshadweep**
- The Union Territory that is under the jurisdiction of Bombay High Court – **Daman and Diu and Dadra and Nagar Haveli**
- The first High Courts were set up in India – **in 1862 (at Calcutta, Madras and Bombay)**
- The High Court that has the lowest number of judges – **Guwahati High Court**
- The High Court that has the highest number of judges – **Allahabad High Court**
- The High Court with broadest jurisdiction – **Guwahati High Court**
- Delhi High Court established in – **1966**
- Patna High Court was established in – **1916**

- Allahabad High Court was established – **1866**
- The age of retirement for the judges of High Courts and Supreme Court – **65 years**
- The official language of High Courts and Supreme Court – **English**
- The division of legislative powers between the center and the states is based on – **the Act of 1935**
- The constitution of Jammu and Kashmir was implemented in – **1957**
- The duration of the Jammu and Kashmir Legislative Assembly is – **6 years**
- The first session of the Jammu and Kashmir Constituent Assembly was convened on – **30th October, 1951**
- How many districts are in Pakistan Occupied Kashmir – **3**
- When was the Governor's Rule first imposed in Jammu and Kashmir – **27th March, 1977**
- Which Article provides the status of Special State Jammu and Kashmir – **Article 370**
- The 'Lee Commission' for the Union Services was formed in – **1923**
- P. K. Thurang Committee was formed in – **1988**
- Lord Rippon established Local Self-rule in the year – **1882**
- Ashok Mehta Committee was formed in – **1977 (13 members)**
- Ashok Mehta Committee was formed in – **1977 (13 members)**
- What was known as Super Cabinet – **Planning Commission (now NITI Commission)**
- Who defines the financial relations between the states and the center – **Finance Commission**
- The old Finance Committee – **Public Audit Committee**
- The chairman of first Finance Commission – **K. C. Niyogi**
- The provision for the formation of Inter-state Council (1990) is mentioned in – **Article 263**
- The number of members of in the Public Audit Committee – **22 (15 from Lok Sabha, 7 from Rajya Sabha)**
- The provision for Union Judiciary is mentioned in – **Article 124 to 147**
- Article 343 is related to – **the official language of the Union**
- Article 352 is related to – **emergency**
- Which Article provides the right to vote – **Article 326**
- When was the first meeting of the Lok Adalat held – **14th March, 1982 (in Junagadh, Gujrat)**

Fundamental Rights

- Right to equality (Article 14 to 18)
- Right to liberty (Article 19 to 22)
- Right against exploitation (Article 23 to 24)
- Right to religious freedom (Article 25 to 28)
- Right related to culture and education (Article 29 to 30)
- Right to Constitutional remedies (Article 32)

- Which article deals with international peace and security – **Article 51**
- Which Article defines the separation between the executive and the judiciary – **Article 50**
- Who has the right to make law on Residuary Powers – **the Union government**
- What type of corps is UPSC – **an advisory corps**
- Who is the conservator of public money wealth of the country – **Comptroller and Auditor General of India**
- The tenure of Comptroller and Auditor General of India – **6 years from the appointment or 65 years of age**
- When was the Public Service Commission established – **1926**
- Who appoints the members of the UPSC and to whom do they offer their resignation – **President**
- The number of members of the UPSC – **10**
- Election Commission is – **an autonomous constitutional body**
- When were the first elections held – **1951-52**
- Who validates a political party as a national party – **Election Commission**
- First Chief Election Commissioner – **Sukumar Sen**
- By which Amendment the voting age was reduced to 18 years from 21 years – **61st Amendment (1989)**
- When was the national emergency announced for tor the first time – **during Indo-China war (1962)**
- In which year the internal emergency announced due to internal turmoil – **1975**
- The Emergency Fund was established in the year – **1950**
- Which Article is known as the 'Soul of the Constitution' – **Article 32**

- Madras City Corporation was established in the year – **1687**
- The first Lok Adalat was held in – **Gujrat**
- The first Lokyukta was appointed in – **Rajasthan**
- Kaka Kalelkar Commission was formed in the year – **1953**
- The last Viceroy of India – **Lord Mountbatten**
- The total number of committees formed to prepare the constitution of India – **13**
- The number of members in the Drafts Committee – **7**
- Until when the Western and Eastern (now Bangladesh) Pakistan were part of India – **14th August, 1947**
- 'India is a secular country' means – **India treats all religions equally**
- Democracy means – **rule by the people**
- 'Bihar National Language Council' was formed in the year – **1950**
- The Article 14 dealing with equality before law is borrowed from – **Britain**
- Who said 'Directive Principles is a check that can be cashed any time' – **K. T. Shah**
- The only state to implement the Uniform Civil Code is – **Goa**
- Which Article deals with a uniform civil code for the citizens – **Article 44**
- The command issued by the Supreme Court or a High Court regarding the Fundamental Rights of the citizens is a – **mandamus (mandatory command)**
- The command that compels the police to bring the prisoner to appear before the court within 24 hours of his arrest is called – **Habeas Corpus**
- The Right to Information Bill was passed in the year – **2005**
- One of the activists trying for the Right to Information is – **Aruna Roy**
- Who appoints the members of the All India Services – **President**
- Who swears-in the judges of the Supreme Court – **Chief Justice of India**
- Who swears-in the Governors – **the Chief Justice of the respective High Court**
- When was Hindi adopted as the language of the Union – **on 14th September, 1949**
- The official languages of the UNO – **English and French**
- The number of members at the UNO at present – **193 (Sudan is the 193rd member)**
- The number of permanent and non-permanent members at the Security Council of the UN – **5 and 10 respectively**
- The body of the UN responsible for world peace – **the Security Council**
- The first woman chairman of the UN General Assembly – **Vijaya Lakshmi Pandit**
- The five permanent members of the UN Security Council are – **China, France, Britain, Russia, USA**
- The headquarter of UN is located at – **New York (Manhattan Island)**
- The chief judicial body of the UN is – **International Court**
- The first General-Secretary of the UN was – **Trygvelie (Norway)**
- The International Court was established on – **3rd April, 1946 (headquarter at Hague, Netherlands)**
- The tenure of the judge of the International Court is – **9 years**
- The first Vice-Chairman of Rajya Sabha – **Anantshayman Ayangar**
- By which amendment the Bodo, Maithili, Dongri and Santhali languages were incorporated in the 8th Schedule of the Constitution – **92nd Amendment (2003)**
- The Objectives Resolution was accepted on – **22nd January, 1947**
- POTA (Prevention of Terrorism Ordinance) was implemented on – **25th October, 2001**
- The Declaration Human Rights was passed at the UN in the year – **1948**
- Who determines whether a bill is Money Bill or not at the state level – **the Speaker of the Vidhan Sabha**
- The national flag was accepted by the Constituent Assembly on – **22nd July, 1947**
- The members of the Cabinet Mission were – **Sir Stafford Cripps, Lord Patrick Lawrence and A. B. Alexander**
- The Press Council was established in – **1956**
- How many writs can the Supreme Court and the High Court issue – **Five (Habeas Corpus, Mandamus, Certiorari, Prohibition and Quo Warranto)**
- The Governors of the states are answerable to – **the President**
- The only Union Territory that has its own High Court – **Delhi**
- When was the Shaka Panchang was adopted – **22nd March, 1957**

- The first and last months of the Shaka Panchang are – **Chaitra and Falgun respectively**
- The Mandal Commission was related to – **the provision of reservation for the backward castes**
- The Solicitor General of India is – **an administrative officer**
- The main aspect of the Government of India Act, 1935 was – **regional self-rule**
- The Jan-Gan-Man was accepted the national anthem on – **24th January, 1950**
- The Jan-Gan-Man was first sung on – **27th December, 1911 (at the Calcutta session of the Congress)**
- The Vande Matram was first sung in – **1896 (at the Calcutta session of the Congress)**
- The financial emergency remains in effect for the first time – **for 6 months**
- The number of members in the Legislative Council can be – **maximum one third of the members of Vidhan Sabha, 40 minimum**
- The tenure of the Legislative Council and Vidhan Sabha is – **6 and 5 years respectively**
- Nagaland was made a separate state by – **13th Amendment (1962)**
- Who defined the Preamble before the Drafts Committee of the Constituent Assembly – **Jawaharlal Nehru**

NITI Aayog

- The National Institution for Transforming India, also called NITI Aayog, was formed via a resolution of the Union Cabinet on January 1, 2015 to replace the Planning Commission which followed a top-down model.
- The Prime Minister is the Ex-officio chairman. The permanent members of the governing council are all the state Chief Ministers, the chief ministers of Delhi and Puducherry, the Lieutenant Governor of Andaman and Nicobar, and a vice chairman nominated by the Prime Minister. In addition, temporary members are selected from leading universities and research institutions. These members include a chief executive officer, four ex-official members and two part-time members.
- The first meeting of NITI Aayog was chaired by Narend ra Modi on 8 February 2015.

Major Constitutional Amendments	
1st (1951)	The Land Reform laws of the states were placed in the 9th Schedule, thus placing them outside the jurisdiction of the courts
7th (1956)	The states were created on linguistic basis and then they were designated as States and Union Territories
21st (1967)	Sindhi language was assimilated into the 8th Schedule as the 15th language
36th (1975)	Sikkim was given the full status as a state
42nd (1976)	The words Socialist, Secular and Integrity were added into the Preamble.
44th (1978)	The Fundamental Right to Property was abolished. The President shall announce emergency in case of an armed mutiny on advice from the Cabinet.
52nd (1985)	Anti-defection Law
61st (1989)	The age of voting was reduced to 18 years from 21 years
65th (1990)	Under it, the Article 338 was amended and SCST Commission was given the constitutional sanctity.
71st (1992)	Konkani, Manipuri and Nepali languages were assembled in the 8th Schedule.
73rd (1992-93)	Panchayti Raj was implemented.
85th (2001)	Reservation in promotion for SC, ST government employees
86th (2002)	The states were to provide free and quality education to all children between 6-14 years of age.
91st (2003)	Anti-defection Law was amended, the defection of the whole political party was legalized. The total number of ministers cannot exceed to more than 15% of total members in the Lok Sabha and the Vidhan Sabha.
92nd (2003)	Bodo, Dongri, Maithili and Santhali languages were assimilated into the 8th Schedule of the constitution.
93rd (2006)	Reservation for educationally and socially backward classes in private and non-government funded educational institutions
109th (Bill)	The reservation for SCs, STs and Anglo-Indians was extended for 10 more years in the Lok Sabha and state Vidhan Sabhas with effect from 26th January, 2010
101st 1 July 2017	Introduced the Goods and Services Tax.

Indian Economy

- The father of economics–**Adam Smith**
- India economy is – **Developing**
- The term 'Third World' is used for – **The developing countries**
- The nations that adopted capitalist and socialist models of economy – **USA and Russia**
- The world's largest economy is – **USA**
- The world's second largest economy is – **China**
- The place of India in the world in terms of Gross Domestic Product – **10th**
- The place of India in the world economy (in terms of purchasing power) – **3rd**
- The place of India in Global Competitiveness Index – **40th**

The Plans for Poverty and Unemployment Eradication and their Starting Years

Plans	Beginning
Desert Development Program	1977-78
Food for Work Program	1977-78
Antyodya Plan Program	1977-78
TRYSEM	1979
DWCRA	1980
Jawahar Employment Scheme	1982
Nehru Employment Scheme	1989
One Million Wells Scheme	1989
Indira Housing Scheme	1988-89
Prime Minister Rozgar Yojna	1985-86
Employment Assurance Scheme	1993
Swarn Jayanti Shahri Rozgar Yojna	1993
Swarn Jayanti Gram Svrozgar Yojna	1997
Pradhan Mantri Jan Dhan Yojana	2014
Pradhan Mantri Mudra Yojana (Pmmy)	2015
Pradhan Mantri Jeevan Jyoti Bima Yojana (Pmjjby)	2015
Pradhan Mantri Fasal Bima Yojana (Pmfby)	2016
Sankalp Se Siddhi	2017
"Shadi Shagun" Scheme	2017
Pradhan Mantri Sahaj Bijli Har Ghar Yojana	2017
Khelo India Scheme 2017-18	2017-18

- The first country to adopt mixed economy model – **France**
- The Indian economic model is – **Mixed economy**
- Mixed economy means – **The coexistence of private and public sector in economy**
- The mixed economy model was adopted in the year – **1948**
- Who conducts the Human Development Report – **UNDP, since 1990**
- The basis for Human Development Index (HDI) is – **Life expectancy, level of education and per capita income**
- The place of India in Human Development Affairs in the HDI-2016 – **131st (out of 188 countries)**
- The first and last countries in the world in the HDI-2016 – **Norway and Central African Republic respectively**
- The first Human Development Report was issued by India in the year – **April, 2002**
- Who issues the Human Development Report of India – **The Planning Commission (NITI Aayog)**
- The first India state to issue the state-level Human Development Report – **Madhya Pradesh**
- The first-ever estimation of national income was done by – **Dada Bhai Nouroji (in 1868)**
- The National Income Committee was formed in – **August, 1949**
- The National Income Committee submitted its first report in – **1951**
- National income is – **A flow, not a stock**
- Hindu Growth Rate is related to – **National income**
- Who was the proponent of the concept of Hindu Growth Rate – **Prof. Raj Krishna**
- The best indicator of the economic development rate of a country is – **Per capita income**
- The first-ever governmental estimate of national income was given in the year – **1948-49**
- The best indicator of national income – **The Net National Product on Factor Cost**
- The major source of India's national income – **Agriculture**
- Who keeps the accounts of the National Income and GDP – **CSO**

- Central Statisstical Organization (CSO) was established on – **2nd May, 1951**
- The CSO conducted the first nationwide economic census in– **1977**
- The headquarter of CSO is located in – **Kolkata**
- The state with the highest share in the GDP – **Maharashtra**
- National Accounts Statistics is also known as – **White-Paper**
- The base year for the estimate of national income at present is– **2011-12**
- Central Statistical Organization is located at – **New Delhi**
- The share of Primary Sector (agriculture), Secondary Sector (industry) and Tertiary Sector (service) in 2016-17 GDP – **17.32%, 29.02% and 53.66% respectively**
- The biggest contributing sector in the GDP is – **Tertiary (service) Sector**
- The Primary Sector is comprised of – **Agriculture, animal husbandry, fisheries**
- The Secondary Sector is comprised of – **Manufacturing, electricity, water availability**
- The Tertiary Sector is comprised of – **Service sector, trade, transportation, communication**
- The leading country in the field of per capita income – **Qatar**
- The leading state and Union Territory in India in terms of per capita income – **Delhi and Goa respectively**
- The marker of measuring poverty in India – **The metric scale of minimum calorie consumption**
- How many minimum calories should an adult consume in the rural and urban areas – **2400 and 2100 calories respectively**
- The poverty is measured is in India according to – **The Lakadwala formula**
- The Lakadwala Formula was accepted on – **11th March, 1997**
- The purpose of the Antodya Program is – **To help the poorest of the poor**
- The Antodya Program was first started in – **Rajasthan**
- Who collects the unemployment related statistics in India – **National Sample Survey Organization**
- The kind of unemployment prevalent in the agriculture sector of India – **Hidden unemployment**

Theories and their Proponents	
The Theory of Development	Dada Bhai Nouroji
The Vicious Circle of Poverty, the Theory of Hidden Unemployment, the Theory of Balanced Development	Ragnar Nurkse
Planning and the Poor	V. S. Minhas
An Enquiry into the Poverty of Nations	Adam Smith
Big Push Model	Paul Rosenstein -Rodan
Unbalanced Development Theory	Albert O. Hirschman
Stages of Economic Growth	Rostov
Collective Choice and Social Welfare	A. K. Sen
Ability to Pay Theory	Adam Smith
Optimum Taxation Theory	Arthur Laffer
Expenditure Tax	Nicholas Kaldor
Tobin Tax	James Tobin
Value Added Tax (VAT)	F. Vaughan Simmons (first proponent)
Value Added Tax (VAT)	Maurice Laure and Karlsruhe (developed)
The Theory of Minimum Sacrifice	J. S. Mill
Zero Base Budgeting	Pete Pyhrr
The Theory of Maximum Social Welfare	Dalton Pigeau
Tax Payment Capacity	Clarke
The Theory of Functional Finance	P. Learner
Compensatory Fiscal Theory	John Maynard Keynes

- The kind of unemployment observed at the time of the depression in the trade cycle – **Cyclical unemployment**
- The form of unemployment in India is – **Structural**
- The kind of unemployment observed in the rural areas – **Seasonal unemployment (in agriculture sector)**
- The kind of unemployment observed in the urban areas– **Visible unemployment**
- The tenure of a Fiscal Year – **1st April to 31st March**
- The establishment of the first Fiscal Commission – **In 1951**

- The Fiscal Commission is established by – **The President (under Article 280)**
- The first Chairman of the Fiscal Commission – **K. C. Niyogi**
- Who appoints the chairman of the Fiscal Commission – **President**
- The number of members in the Fiscal Commission – **5 (including the Chairman)**
- The total number of Fiscal Commissions established so far – **15**
- The 15th Fiscal Commission was established in the year – **2017**
- The time period for the recommendations of the 14th Fiscal Commission is – **From 2020 to 2025**
- The Chairman of 15th Fiscal Commission – **N. K. Singh**
- The chief function of the Finance Comm-ission is – **To determine revenue distribution between the states and the center**
- The Chairman of the 7th Pay Commission – **AK Mathur**
- Planning Commission was established on – **15th March, 1951**
- The proposal for the establishment of the Planning Commission was presented by– **John Mathai (in 1950)**
- Planning Commission was established on the recommendations of – **Niyogi Committee (1946)**
- Planning Commission is an – **Advisory and non-constitutional body**
- The chairman of the Planning Commission is – **Prime Minister**
- The first Chairman and Vice-Chairman of the Planning Commission were – **Jawaharlal Nehru and Gulzarilal Nanda respectively**
- The Vice-Chairman of the Planning Commission is designated the status of a – **Cabinet minister**
- Who appoints the Vive-Chairman of the Planning Commission – **Prime Minister with consultation with the President**
- The number of members of the Planning Commission and their tenure – **Not defined (variable)**
- The chief task of the Planning Commission is – **To prepare the blueprint of the Five-Year Plans**
- When did the Planning Commission prepare its India Vision 2020 document – **23rd January, 2003**
- The target GDP suggested in India Vision 2020 document is – **9%**
- Which body is known as 'Super Cabinet' – **Niti Aayog**
- National Development Council (NDC) was established on –**6th August, 1952**
- NDC is a – **Non-constitutional body**
- The Chairman of NDC–**Prime Minister**
- The members of NDC include – **Members of the central cabinet, Chief Ministers of the states, the administrators of the Union Territories and the members of the Planning Commission**
- The nature of planning in India is – **Mixed**
- 'Planned Economy for India' is written by – **M. Visvesvaraya (in 1934)**
- The writer of the 'Gandhian Plan' – **Shriman Narayan Agarwal (in 1944)**
- 'Bombay Plan' (15-year plan) was executed in– **1944 (by 8 industrialists)**
- People's Plan was expounded by – **M. N. Rai (in April, 1945)**
- Sarvodaya Plan was expounded by – **Jai Prakash Narayan (in January, 1950)**
- Planning means – **Economic employment**
- The first country to adopt economic planning – **Soviet Russia**
- Economic planning is the subject of which List of the Indian Constitution – **Union List**
- The Schedule related to economic planning – **7th Schedule**
- The beginning of planned economic development – **In 1951**
- Who is responsible for the execution of Five-Year Plans in India – **The central and the state governments**
- National Planning Committee was established in the year – **1938**
- The Chairman of the National Planning Committee – **Jawaharlal Nehru**
- National Planning Committee submitted its report in the year – **1949**
- The Five-Year Plans of India are inspired by – **Soviet Russia**
- The first Five-Year Plan (1951-56) was based on – **Harrod-Domar Model**
- Which sector was given preference in the first Five-Year Plan – **Agriculture**
- The second Five-Year Plan was based on – **P. C. Mahalanobis Model**

- Which sector was given the top priority in the second Five-Year Plan – **Heavy and basic industries**
- Raurkela (Odisha), Bhilai (Chhatisgadh) and Durgapur (West Bengal) steel plants were established during – **The second Five-Year Plan**
- Jawaharlal Nehru gave the slogan of 'more work, more production and greater redistribution' during – **The second Five-Year Plan**
- The third Five-Year Plan was based on – **Domer Growth Model**
- The objective of the third Five-Year Plan was – **To make the economy self-reliant and automatic**
- The least successful Five-Year Plan – **The third Five-Year Plan**
- The target development rate and actually achieved growth rate of the third Five-Year Plan was – **5.6% and 2.8% respectively**
- The main reasons for the failure of the third Five-Year Plan– **Indo-China war (1962), Indo- Pak war (1965) and widespread famine**
- The three yearly plans were executed in the year – **From 1966-69**
- The three yearly plans have been termed as – **The Plan Holidays of 1966-69**
- The Green Revolution and the Bokaro Steel Plant were established during – **The Plan Holidays**
- The time-period for the fourth Five-Year Plan – **1969-74**
- Who prepared the blueprint for the fourth Five-Year Plan – **D. R. Gadgil**
- The new institute established in place of the Planning Commission – **NITI Ayog**
- The Gadgil Plan is known as – **The Fourth Plan**
- The objective of the fourth Five-Year Plan was – **Stable development**
- The time-period for the fifth Five-Year Plan was – **1974-79**
- Who prepared the blueprint for the fifth Five-Year Plan – **D. P. Dhar**
- The chief objective of the fifth Five-Year Plan was – **Poverty eradication and self-sufficiency**
- The Five-Year Plan that got completed 1 year in advance of its designated time-frame - **The fifth Plan**
- Indira Gandhi gave the slogan "Garibi Hatao' during – **The fifth Five-Year Plan**
- 'Food for Work' program (1977-78) was initiated during – **The fifth Five-Year Plan**
- National Minimum Need Program (NMNP, 1974) was initiated during – **The fifth Five-Year Plan**
- The time-period of the Rolling Plan – **1978-80**
- The proponent of the Rolling Plan – **Gunnar Myrdal**
- Who developed the Rolling Plan – **Ragnar Frisch**
- The Rolling Plan is based on – **The Gandhian Model**
- NABARD was established during – **The sixth Five-Year Plan (1980-85)**
- National Rural Employment Plan was initiated during –**The sixth Five-Year Plan**
- Who prepared the blueprint for the seventh Five-Year Plan – **Ramakrishna Hegde**
- Indira Housing Scheme (1985-86) and Jawahar Employment Scheme (28th April, 1989) were started during – **The seventh Five-Year Plan**
- Who prepared the blueprint for the eighth Five-Year Plan – **Pranab Mukherjee**
- The chief objective of the eighth Five-Year Plan – **The development of the human resource**
- The most successful Five-Year Plan so far – **The eighth Plan**
- The Target Development rate and actual Development rate of the eighth Five-Year Plan – **5.6% and 6.8% respectively**
- Woman Growth Plan (2nd October, 1993) was started during – **The eighth Plan**
- The chief objective of the ninth Five-Year Plan was – **Economic growth with social justice and equality**
- The time-period for the tenth Plan – **2002-07**
- The Plan that achieved the fastest development rate – **The tenth Plan**
- The Target development rate and actual development rate of the tenth Plan – **8% and 7.6% respectively**

Important Committees	
Swaminathan Committee	Population Policy
Jankiraman Committee	Securities Scam
Dantawala Committee	Estimation of poverty
Rekhi Committee	Indirect taxes
Sarkaria Committee	Center-State relations
Goswami Committee	Industrial sickness
Mahalanobis Committee	National Income
Rangarajan Committee	Balance of Payments
Raja Chelaiya Committee	Tax reforms
Malhotra Committee	Reforms in the Insurance Sector
Khusrau Committee	Agricultural Credit
Goiporia Committee	Reforms in the Banking Sector
Bhurelal Committee	Increase in the taxes on motor vehicles
Narsimhan Committee	Fiscal (banking) reforms
Bhandari Committee	Restructuring of the Regional Rural banks
Sachchar Committee	The study of social, economic and educational status of the Muslims
Suresh Tendulkar Committee	Poverty
S. Tarapore Committee	The convertibility of Rupee in the Capital Account
Abid Hussain Committee	Small industry
Dr. Kirit Shantilal Committee	Suggestion on the price system of the petroleum products

- The time-period for the 11th Five-Year Plan – **2007-12**
- The main objective of the 11th Five-Year Plan – **To increase the Economic Growth Rate**
- The time-period for the 12th Five-Year Plan – **2012-17**
- Antodaya Foodgrain Scheme was initiated on – **25th December, 2000**
- Annapurna Scheme was initiated on – **1st April, 2000**
- TRYSEM Scheme was initiated on – **15th August, 1979**
- Twenty Point Program was initiated in – **1974-75**
- National Rural Employment Scheme (NREP) was initiated in – **1980**
- Sampoorna Gramin Rozgar Yojna (SGRY) was initiated on – **25th September, 2001**
- National Rural Employment Guarantee Act (NREGA) was passed on – **2nd February, 2006**
- NAREGA was started at – **In the Ananatpur district of Andhra Pradesh by Prime Minister Manmohan Singh**
- Mahatma Gandhi National Rural Employment Guarantee Act (MNREGA) was started on – **2nd October, 2009 (in place of NAREGA)**
- Jawahar Gram Samriddhi Yojna was started on – **1st April, 1999**
- Sarva Shiksha Abhiyan was started on – **2000-01**
- Hariyali Yojna was started on – **27th January, 2003**
- Farmer Insurance Income Scheme was started in – **2003-04**
- Sva-Jaldhar Karyakram was started in – **December, 2002**
- Pradhan Mantri Gram Sadak Yojna was started in – **December, 2000**
- Pradhan Mantri Gramodaya Yojna was started in – **2000-01**
- Prime Minister Employment Generation Program started on – **15th August, 2008**
- National Agriculture Insurance Scheme was started in – **1999-2000**
- Development of Women and Children in Rural Areas was started in – **1982**
- CAPART was established on – **1st September, 1986 (headquarters in New Delhi)**
- Who gave the theory of consumer savings – **Alfred Marshal**
- Closed economy means– **An economy that does not import or export**
- 'Minimum Support Price' is related to – **Agriculture**
- The organization that implements the Minimum Support Price – **Commission for Agricultural Costs and Prices (CACP)**
- Consolidation of agricultural land (Chakbandi) law was first implemented in India at– **Baroda (in 1920)**
- Two types of Consolidation – **Voluntary and Compulsory**
- Voluntary Consolidation started at

– **Punjab (in 1921)**
- Compulsory Consolidation started at -**Madhya Pradesh (in 1928)**
- The most prevalent type of land holdings in India – **Marginal land holdings**
- The state with biggest number of small land holdings – **Kerala**
- The state with big land holdings – **Rajasthan**
- The Rabi crops are sowed in the months – **October-November**
- The Kharif crops are sown in the months – **June-July**
- Some major Rabi crops are – **Wheat, barley, grams, peas, mustard**
- Some major Kharif crops are – **Rice, millet, corn**
- Some major Zaid crops are – **Cucumber, watermelon, vegetables**
- The chief food crop of India – **Rice and wheat**
- The first experimenter of Green Revolution in India – **Dr. William Gaud**
- The Green Revolution started in the year – **1966-67**
- Who is credited to have introduced the Green Revolution in India – **Dr. Govind Vallabh Pant University**
- The father of Indian Green Revolution – **M. S. Swaminathan**
- The father of Green Revolution at world level – **Dr. Norman Borlaug**
- The crop most affected by Green Revolution – **Wheat**
- Who was the central Food and Agriculture minister of India at the time of the Green Revolution – **C. S. Subrahmanyam**
- The country where the Green Revolution first started – **Philippines**
- The first state of India to witness the Green Revolution – **Punjab**
- Yellow Revolution is related to – **Oilseeds production**
- Red Revolution is related to – **Tomato and meat production**
- Pink Revolution is related to – **Jhinga (prawns) fish production**
- White Revolution is related to – **Milk production**
- Silver Revolution is related to – **Egg production**
- Almond (brown) Revolution is related to – **Spices production**
- Round Revolution is related to – **Potato production**
- Blue Revolution is related to – **Fish production**
- Black Revolution is related to – **Petroleum production**
- Brown Revolution is related to – **Non-conventional energy production**
- Golden Revolution is related to – **Fruits production**
- The amalgamation of all the revolutions is known as – **Rainbow Revolution**
- Direct Taxes are – **Income tax, property tax, corporation tax, death tax, land revenue tax, gift tax**
- Indirect taxes are– **Sales tax, production tax, excise duty, coast tax**
- The taxes levied by the central government – **Income tax, corporation tax, property tax, money tax, gift tax, excise duty, tax on agricultural property**
- The taxes levied by the state governments – **Land revenue tax, agricultural income tax, sales tax, entertainment tax, motor vehicle tax, toll tax**
- The committee that was established to reform the tax system – **Chelaiya Committee (established August, 1991)**
- The major source of the income of the central government–**Corporation tax (direct tax)**

Major Financial and Trade Organizations

Organization	Year
Industrial Finance Corporation of India (IFCI)	1948
State Finance Commission (SFC)	1951
Small Industry Development Organization (SIDO)	1954
Industrial Credit and Investment Corporation of India Bank (ICICI)	1955
Unit Trust of India (UTI)	1964
Industrial Development Bank of India (IDBI)	1964
Indian Tourism Development Corporation (ITDC)	1966
Housing and Urban Development Corporation (HUDCO)	1970
EXIM Bank	1982
Council for Advancement of People's Action and Rural Technology (CAPART)	1986
National Housing Bank (NHB)	1988
Securities and Exchange Board of India (SEBI)	1988
Tourism Finance Corporation of India Limited (TFCI)	1989

Small Industry Development Bank of India (SIDBI)	1990
Food Corporation of India (FCI)	1965
Tea Trade Corporation of India (TTCI)	1971
Metal and Minerals Trade Corporation (MMTC)	1963
Indian Trade Promotion Organization (ITPO)	1982
Life Insurance Corporation of India (LIC)	1956
General Insurance Corporation of India (GIC)	1972
State Bank of India (SBI)	1955
Steel Authority of India Limited (SAIL)	1974
Regional Rural Bank (RRB)	1975
Reserve Bank of India (RBI)	1935
Punjab National Bank (PNB)	1894
Housing Development Finance Corporation (HDFC)	1977
National Bank for Agriculture and Rural Development (NABARD)	1982

- The major source of income for the state governments – **VAT (formerly known as Sales Tax)**
- The center derives maximum revenue from – **Production tax**
- The main source of income for Municipal Corporations– **Octroi duty**
- The number of services registered under the Service Tax – **119**
- The service tax was imposed for the first time in – **1994-95 (on the recommendation of Chelaiya Committee)**
- The time-period and Target Development Rate of the 12th Five-Year Plan is– **2012-2017 and 9% respectively**
- Rekha Committee was established to – **Reform the indirect tax system**
- Vanchu Committee was related to – **Survey of direct taxes**
- Who collects the Service Tax – **Income Tax Department**
- The condition where the price of things increase is called – **Inflation**
- Inflation is measured in India through – **Wholesale price index**
- The current base year for wholesale price index is – **2011-12**
- The number of goods registered in the revised wholesale price index – **697**
- Inflation brings loss to – **The payer or debtor**
- Inflation is profitable to – **The creditor**
- The process of monetizing of fiscal deficit in India – **The government takes debts**
- The Gresham's Law is related to – **Currency circulation**
- Legal Currency is known as – **Flat Money**
- Plastic money is also known as – **Credit card**
- The most liquid measurement of currency supply – **M1**
- The expansive currency in currency supply is known as – **M2**
- Guild Aged Bazaar is related to – **Gold and silver**
- India spends majority of its foreign currency reserve on – **The import of petroleum products**
- India earn majority of its foreign currency from – **The export of jewels and expensive stones**
- Maximum imported product in India – **Oil and petroleum products**
- The first country to adopt metric system of currency– **France (in 1790)**
- The metric system of currency was adopted in India on – **1st April, 1957**
- The objective of currency devaluation is – **Increase the export and decrease in the imports**
- Who provides financial aid to exporters and importers – **Export-Import (Exim) Bank**
- Exim Bank was established on – **1st January, 1982**
- Life insurance in India is adopted from – **Britain**
- The organizations that provides long-term finance – **UTI, LIC, GIC**
- General Insurance Corporation was established in – **1972**
- India's General Insurance industry was nationalized in – **1971**
- Life Insurance Corporation Limited (LIC) was established on – **1st September, 1956**
- The biggest mutual fund trust organization – **UTI**
- Unit Trust of India (UTI) was established on – **1st July, 1964 (headquarter in Mumbai)**
- The first mutual fund of India – **U. S. – 64**
- U. S. – 64 scheme was abolished on – **21st May, 2003**
- NABARD was established on – **12th July, 1982 (on report of Shivaraman Committee)**
- Security Press, Security Printing and Minting Corporation and Bank Note Press of India are located at – **Nasik, Hyderabad and Dewas respectively**

- The structure of government committees in India is – **Trilateral**
- The wage earned in cash is called – **Monetary wage**
- The reserve Bank of India was established on – **1st April, 1935 (nationalized on 1st January, 1949)**
- Reserve Bank of India was established on the recommendation of – **Hilton Commission**
- The biggest public sector business bank of the country – **State Bank of India (SBI), established on 1st July, 1955**
- who made the recommendation that banks should be nationalized – **Hazari Committee**
- 14 big business banks were first nationalized on – **19th July, 1969**
- The second order to nationalize 6 big business banks was implemented on – **15th April, 1980**
- For how many days does the reserve bank offer loans to central and state governments – **90 days**
- The maximum number of branches of India banks outside India are in – **United Kingdom**

Some Regularly Used Vocabulary of the Banking Sector	
Bank Rate	The interest rate at which the Reserve Bank offers loan to the business banks is called 'Bank Rate..
Repo Rate	The rate of interest at which the commercial banks obtain short-term credit loans from the Reserve Bank is called 'Repo Rate.'
Reverse Repo Rate	The rate of interest at which the Reserve Bank obtains short-term credit loans from the commercial banks is called 'Reverse Repo Rate.
Saving Bank Rate	The rate of interest paid to the customers by the bank on the small savings is called 'Saving Bank Rate.'
Credit Rate	The rate of interest paid to the customers on their time-bound savings is called 'Credit rate.'
Cash Reserve Ration (CRR)	The portion of the total credit currency of the commercial banks that they have to deposit with the Reserve Bank is called 'Cash Reserve Ration.
Legal Liquidation Ration (LLR)	The portion of the total credit of a commercial bank that has to be kept reserved in the form of gold or foreign currency is called 'Legal Liquidation Ratio.
Prime Lending Rate (PLR)	Prime Lending rate is the rate of interest at which the bank is ready to provide loan to a customer with zero percent risk. This rate actually functions as basic rate of interest.

- The first commercial bank to issue Prepaid Cards – **Oriental Bank of Commerce**
- Narsimhan Committee is related to – **Banking reforms**
- Goiporia Committee is related to – **Customer service reform in banking**
- The first mobile bank of the country – **Lakshmi Vahini Bank (Madhya Pradesh)**
- The first floating ATM of the country was established by – **SBI (in Kochi)**
- The new name of the U. T. Bank Limited with effect from 30th July, 2007 is – **Axis Bank Limited**
- The rate at which the RBI provides loans to the registered banks is called – **Bank Rate**
- The portion of credit defined by the RBI that the commercial banks have to keep reserved with themselves is called – **Legal Liquidation Ration (LLR)**
- The portion of credit defined by the RBI that the commercial banks have to keep with the RBI is called – **Cash Reserve Ratio (CRR)**
- The cooperative banks were started in India in the year – **1904**
- The RBI declares monetary policy – **For the next six months**
- Industrial Development Bank of India (IDBI) was established on – **1st February, 1964**
- 'A Gamble on the Monsoon' is referred to – **Indian budget**
- The pre-budget economic analysis is presented before – **The Lok Sabha only**
- Deficit Budget means– **When government expenditure exceeds its income**
- The Law of the Market theory was expounded by – **J. B. Say**
- Sarkaria Commission was established in – **1983, by the Parliament**

Major Industrial Organizations of India	
Organization	**Location**
Hindustan Machine tools Corp.	Bengaluru (Karnataka)
Indian Iron and Steel Co.	Bernpur (West Bengal)
Bokaro Steel Limited	Bokaro (Jharkhand)
Hindustan Steel Limited	Raurkela (Odisha)
Hindustan Shipyard Ltd.	Kochin (Kerala)
Bharat Heavy Electricals Ltd.	Bhopal (M. P.)
Integral Coach Factory	Perumbudur (Tamilnadu)
Currency Note Press	Nasik (Maharashtra)
Hindustan Aircraft Inst.	Bengaluru (Karnataka)

- The headquarter of NSE is located at – **Varli, South Mumbai**
- NIFTY adopts the value index of – **NSE**
- The Bull and Bear terminology is related to – **Share market**
y
- The biggest industry of India is – **Cotton cloth industry**
- The biggest industry of the world – **Tourism**
- The first iron-steel factory was established in the year – **1907 (in Sankchi, Jamshedpur)**
- The number of Maharatna and Navaratna companies in India – **7 and 14 respectively**
- Core sector means – **Selective basic industry**
- The industries of the core sector are – **Cement, iron, steel, petroleum, heavy machinery etc.**
- NTPC was established in – **1975**
- ONGC was established in – **1956**
- The first state fiscal corporation was established in – **1953 (in Punjab)**
- ISI certification was first issued in – **7th April, 2003**
- Hallmark is related to – **Gold jewelry**
- Hallmark scheme was started on – **12th April, 2002**
- Eco-mark is provided to – **The product that does not harm ecosystem**
- Eco-marks were first decided for – **Soaps and detergents**
- Credit Rating Information Service of India Limited (CRISIL) is – **A credit rating agency**
- What denotes the quality of agricultural products – **Ag-mark**
- National ag-mark laboratory is located at – **Nagpur**
- The Patent Act was passed in India in – **1970**
- Trademark Act is effective from – **15th September, 2003**
- SAIL was established in – **1974**
- White Gold is referred to as – **Cotton**
- The Golden Liquid is referred to as – **Petroleum**
- The Big Push Theory was given by – **Rodan**

Indian Tax System

Tax	Related Sector
Direct Tax	Income tax, property tax, gift tax, corporation tax, land revenue, death tax
Indirect tax	Sales tax, coast tax, production tax, excise duty
Central government	Income tax, corporation tax, property tax, inheritance tax, money tax, gift tax, excise duty, agriculture tax
State government	Land revenue, agricultural income tax, agricultural holding tax, sates tax, state production duty, entertainment tax, stamp duty, toll tax, motor vehicle tax

Standardization Certificates

ISO-9001	For quality management
ISO-14001	For environmental management
ISO-22000	For food safety
ISO-27001	For security purposes
ISO 9202	For purity of the jewelry
ISO-18001	Commercial, health and security management certification process
ISO-15700	Priceless services quality management certification process

Direct taxes of the central government	Income tax, corporation tax, money tax, estate duty, expenditure tax
Direct taxes of the state government	Land revenue, tax on hotel returns, agricultural income tax, business tax, employment tax
Indirect taxes of the central government	Central production tax, service tax, excise tax, central sales tax
Indirect taxes of the state government	Sales tax, state production tax, motor vehicle tax, entry tax, advertisement tax, education sub-tax, tax on raw jute, electricity tax, stamp and registration duty, diesel and petrol tax

PHYSICS

Unit

Unit: The measurement index of a quantity is called unit.

Units are of two kind: fundamental unit and derived unit.

Kilogram, meter, candela, second, ampere Kalvin and mole are fundamental units.

1 Light Year = 9.46×10^{15} meter

The biggest unit of distance is Parsec.

1 Parsec = 3.26 Light Years = 3.08×10^{16} m

In the C.G.S system the unit of force is Dyne and in S.I system the unit of force is Newton. 1 newton = 10^5 Dyne.

In the C.G.S system the unit of work done is Erg and in the S.I system the unit is Joule. 1 Joule = 10^7 Erg

Work, Power and Energy

Work is equal to the multiplication of force and the displacement of the object in the direction of the force. Work = Force × Displacement of the object in the direction of force

The rate of work done is called Power. Power is a scalar quantity, its unit of measurement if Watt.

1 Watt hour = 3600 Joules

1 Kilo Watt hour = 3.6×10^6 Joules

1 Horse Power = 746 Watts

> **Isaac Newton**, the Father of Physics, propagated the laws motion for the first time in his book **'Principia.'**
>
> **First Law:** an object will remain at rest or in uniform motion in a straight line unless acted upon by an external force. This law is also called the **Law of Galileo or the Law of Inertia.**
>
> **Second Law:** the acceleration of an object as produced by a net force is directly proportional to the magnitude of the net force, in the same direction as the net force and inversely proportional to the mass of the object.
>
> **Third Law:** for every action there is an equal and opposite reaction.
>
> The tendency of an object to remain static or to maintain constant motion in absence of an external force is called **Inertia.**

An object's capacity to perform a task is called the energy of that object. Energy is a scalar quantity, its unit of measurement is Joule.

- The body that circulates around a planet is called the **satellite** of that planet.

Motion

- **Scalar quantity**: A physical quantity that has magnitude but no direction. E. g. motion, work etc.
- **Vector quantity**: A physical quantity that has magnitude as well as direction of movement. It is added through rules of addition.
- **Distance**: The length traveled by an object in a given time is called Distance. It is always +ve.
- **Displacement**: The horizontal (minimum) distance between two objects in a certain direction.
- **Motion**: The distance covered by an object per second. Its S.I unit is M/S^2
- **Velocity**: The rate of displacement of an object or the distance traveled by an object in a certain direction per second. Its S.I unit is M/S
- **Acceleration**: The rate of change in the velocity of an object. Its S.I unit is M/ S^2

Gravity

- The force that attracts a body towards any other body having mass is called Gravity.
- Gravity is the force by which the earth pulls the objects toward its center.
- The scale of Gravitational Acceleration (g) on moon is 1/6th of the Gravitational Acceleration of the earth.

$$G = 6.67\times10^{-11}\ \frac{Nm^2}{Kg^2}$$

$$g = 9.8\,m/s^2$$

- If a simple pendulum is to be taken to the moon from the earth its periodic season increases because the moon has less Gravitational Acceleration.
- The acceleration that is generated due to gravity is called Gravitational Acceleration (g). Its value is **$9.8M/S^2$**

- **Angular Velocity**: If a particle is circling around a center then the line that joins that particle to the center makes an angle. The angle that lines makes in a second is called the Angular Velocity of that particle. Linear Motion = Angular Motion × Radius
- Moon is the natural satellite of the earth.
- The orbital motion of a satellite does not depend on its mass. The motion of satellites with varying masses will be the same in the orbit of a radius.
- The orbital motion of a satellite depends on the orbital radius. The orbital motion of a satellite circling close to the earth's surface is estimated to be 7.9 or 8 KM/S.
- The orbital period of the satellite circling close to the earth's surface is 84 minutes.
- Geostationary satellites circle around the earth from a distance of 36000 KM for the earth's surface.
- This satellite orbits along the axis of the earth from west to east and its rotational period is equal to the rotational period of the earth, i.e. 24 hours

The Escape Velocity is the minimum speed needed for an object to break free from the gravity of earth. Once the objects reaches beyond the gravity of earth, it does not return back. Its value is 11.2 KM/S on the surface of the earth.

Escape Velocity is $\sqrt{2}$ times of the orbital velocity.

The Escape Velocity on the moon is 2.38 KM/S, this is why there is no atmosphere on the moon.

Counterforce

The force applied at per unit area is called Counterforce. Its unit is Newton m^2 or Pascal.

Deformity

The change in shape or size of an object is called Deformity.

The ratio of counterforce and deformity is called Elasticity Multiple.

If the deformity and the counterforce is longitudinal, then the Elasticity Multiple is called **Young Elasticity Multiple.**

According to snell's law when a light ray passes from one medium to another the angle of incidence to the angle of refraction is constant

Pressure

The force applied at per unit area of a surface is called Pressure.

Its unit is Newton/M^2. It is a vector quantity.

Atmospheric pressure is measured with a **Barometer.**

Hydraulic lift, hydraulic press and hydraulic brake etc. are based on **Pascal's Law.**

The melting point of an object increases as the pressure increases.

The objects whose volume decreases after heating, their melting point also decreases under pressure.

The boiling point of all the liquids increases as the pressure decreases.

Archimedes' Principle

When an object is dipped into liquid, its weight decreases. This illusionary decrease is equal to the mass of the liquid displaced by the object.

Density

- Mass per unit volume is called Density.
- Relative density is measured with hydrometer.
- The density of the ocean water is more than that of the clean water.

Surface Tension

- If liquid's temperature is increased, the surface tension decreases and critical temperature becomes zero.
- The unit of surface tension id Newton/M.
- The surface tension of clean water is higher than that of the soapy water. The surface tension of soapy water can be reduced by mixing it with clean water.
- The force that attracts different atoms of a substance is called Cohesive Force. Whereas the force that attracts the atoms of different substances is called Adhesive Force.
- It is because of the Adhesive Force that water drenches other things and mercury does not attach to glass.

Capillary Action

The process by which the liquid goes up or down in a test tube is called Capillary Action.

Bernoulli's Theorem

- When a liquid flows inside a test tube in a linear motion, then the total of energy (pressure energy; static energy and kinetic energy) pressure at its volume remains constant on every point of its journey.
- Venturimeter, Bunsen burner, carbon filter pump, Magnus effect and the speed of the aeroplane are based on Bernoulli's Theorem.

Simple Pendulum

A spherule hanged with a cord attached to a firm base is called a Simple Pendulum.

The rotation period T= $2\pi\sqrt{\frac{l}{g}}$

The maximum rotational period of the pendulum is 84.6 minutes.

Wave

- Wave is an oscillation that transfers energy from one place to another.
- Wave are of two types: 1) Mechanical Waves (Longitudinal Waves and Transverse Waves) and 2) Electro-Magnetic Waves

Types of Waves

- **Longitudinal Waves:** particles of the medium are displaced in a direction parallel to the direction of energy transport. Sound waves are an example of longitudinal waves.
- **Transverse Waves:** particles of the medium are displaced in a direction perpendicular to the direction of energy transport. Waves generated on the surface of the water and light waves are examples of transverse waves.
- **Electro-Magnetic Waves:** these waves do not require a medium for travelling. Light and heat are examples of electro-magnetic waves. These waves travel with the speed of light.

Sound Waves

- Sound travels from one place to another in the form of waves.
- Sound waves are **longitudinal waves.**
- Sound waves have mainly three frequency ranges:

1. **Audible Waves:** the waves between the ranges of **20 Hertz to 20000 Hertz** are called Audible Waves. We can listen to these waves with our ears.
2. **Infrasonic Waves:** the sound waves below the range of 20 Hertz are called Infrasonic Waves. We cannot listen to these waves with our ears.
3. **Ultrasonic Waves:** the sound wave with the range of over 20000 Hertz are called Ultrasonic Waves. Human ears cannot listen these waves but cats, dogs and mosquitos can listen to these waves. Bats can even produce these waves.

The Use of Ultrasonic Waves:

1. Sending signals
2. Measurement of sea level
3. Repairing of expensive clothes, airplane and watch parts.
4. Cleaning the chimneys of factories
5. Destroying the pathogens in milk
6. Helps bats to navigate in darkness
7. Curing arthritis and detection of brain tumor

Heat

- Heat is an energy that makes us feel the warmth of objects.
- Its unit is Calorie, Kilo Calorie and Jules.
- 1 calories = 4.186 Jules

Temperature

- Temperature is the measurement of warmth and coldness of an object.
- Thermometer is used to measure the temperature.
- The average temperature of human body is 37°c or 98.4°F
- °C and °F become equal at -40°c
- The medical thermometer measures temperature from 96°F to110°F.

$$\frac{C}{5} = \frac{F-32}{9} = \frac{R}{4} = \frac{K-273}{5} = \frac{Ra-49.2}{9}$$

- The freezing point of mercury is -39°c and the freezing point of alcohol is -25°c.

Specific Heat

- Specific heat is the amount of heat that causes a specific amount of heat in the per unit mass of an object.
- Its unit is Jules or KG Kalvin.
- Water has the highest specific heat.
- Most of the objects register increase in specific heat as the temperature increases.
- The specific heat of water decreases until the temperature rises from 0°c to 40°c. After this point, its specific heat increases.

- The specific heat of water at 15°c is 4180Jules/KG–Kalvin.
- Mercury has low specific heat.
- The specific heat of gold is 130 Jules/KG Kalvin.

Latent Heat

- Latent heat is energy released or absorbed by a body during a constant temperature process that is specified in some way.
- The melting latent heat of ice is 80 Jules/KG **Kalvin.**
- The latent heat of evaporation is 540 Calorie/Gram.

Heat Transferring

- The process of the heat traveling from one place to another is called heat Transferring.
- In solid objects, heat transfers through Conduction Process.
- In liquid and gaseous objects, heat transfers through Convection Process.
- The reaches to earth from the sun through Convection Process.

Light

Light is a type of energy that travels in the form of electro-magnetic waves. Light is a Transverse Wave.

Ole Rammer measured the speed of light for the first time. Light travels faster in air and vacuum ($3\times10.^{8}$ M/S).

The sunlight reaches to earth in 8 minutes and 19 seconds.

The process when light collides with a shiny surface and turns back is called Reflection.

Incident ray is perpendicular to Incident Point. Incident ray and Reflected ray fall on the same platform. The Angle of Incidence is always equal to the angle of Reflection.

Reflection from a Plane Mirror

- Reflection is always proportional and inverse to the assumed object.
- If a person walks toward a mirror with v motion then she will feel her reflection to be moving toward her with a speed of 2v.
- To see the full reflection of an object in a plane mirror, the height of the mirror should be half of that of the height of the object.
- The number of reflections formed by plane mirrors: $n = \left(\frac{360°}{\theta} - 1\right)$

Spherical Mirror

- Spherical mirrors are of two type: concave mirror and convex mirror.
- The reflection formed by convex mirror is smaller, straight and virtual than the object whereas the reflection formed by the concave mirror is bigger and real.

Uses of Concave Mirror

- Shaving 2. Used by the ENT doctors 3. Used in motor vehicle headlights 4. In solar cooker

Uses of Convex Mirror

- The rear-view mirror in the vehicles 2. In sodium reflective lamps

Refraction of Light

- When the light ray travels from one medium to another then its trajectory changes its angle. This change in angle is called Refraction.
- The refraction point of red color is lowest and refraction point of violet color is highest.
- When a light ray travels from one medium to another, its frequency remains unchanged while its wavelength and speed changes.

$$\text{Absolute Refractory Point} = \frac{\text{the speed of light in vaccume}}{\text{the speed of light in}}$$

- Generally, refractory point decreases even while the temperature increases.

Lens

- Lens are of two type: convex lens and conclave lens.
- When a lens is dipped into liquid with higher refractory point, its focal length increases and convex lens starts to behave like conclave lens and conclave lens starts to behave like convex lens. Air bubble acts like conclave lens in liquid.

Human Eye: Minimum range of vision is 25 C.M.

Vision Deformities

- **Myopia:** The person afflicted with this deformity can see the nearby objects but cannot see the distant objects. Concave lens is used to help the person see the distant objects.

Photon Theory of Light: light energy travels in small pockets or bundles, these are called Photon.

- **Hypermetropia:** The person afflicted with this disease cannot see the nearby objects. Convex lens is used to cure this deformity.
- **Presbyopia:** The person becomes unable to see the objects both near and distant. Bifocal lens are used to cure this disease.
- **Astigmatism:** The eye can see horizontally but cannot see vertically. Cylindrical lens are used to cure this illness.

The Speed of Light in Various Mediums

Medium	Speed of Light
Vacuum	3×10^8
Glass	2×10^8
Water	2.25×10^8
Rock Salt	1.96×10^8
Turpentine Oil	2.04×10^8
Nylon	1.96×10^8

Charge

- When two matters are rubbed to with each-other then the charge that is produced is called Static Electric Charge.
- **Benjamin Franklin** defined two types of charges: Positive Charge and Negative Charge.
- The charges of same type **retract** while the opposite charges **attract** each other.
- The magnetic field inside a hollow conductor is **zero.**
- **Conductor:** The matter through which the charge can travel easily is called a Conductor. I. e. silver, copper, aluminum etc.
- **Non-Conductor:** The matters through whom the charge cannot travel are called Non-Conductors. I. e. wood, rubber, paper etc.

Electric Current

- The rate of flow of electric charge in conductor is called an Electric Current. Its unit is Ampere. It is a Vector quantity.

Ohm's Law

The potential difference (voltage) across an ideal conductor is proportional to the current through it.

$I = \frac{V}{R}$ where is R is resistance

- In metals, the resistance increases as the temperature increases.
- In semi-conductors, the resistance decreases as the temperature increases.
- In Electric Decompositions, the resistance decreases as the temperature increases.
- The Specific Resistance of the metals depends entirely on their matter.
- If a cord is stretched and its length is doubled, then its resistance changes but its Specific Resistance remains constant.
- The reverse of the Specific Resistance of a conductor is called Conductivity. Its unit is $(\text{Ohm Meter})^1$.
- **Ammeter:** Is the instrument used to measure electric current. It is always arranged in sequential form. The resistance of ideal ammeter is zero.
- **Voltmeter:** Is an instrument used to measure electronic potential in volts. It is always placed in the circuit parallel order. The resistance of an ideal Voltmeter is infinite.
- **Electric Fuse:** it is an electric safety device used to ensure safety of the instruments attached to an electric circuit. It is made from the alloy of tin and glass. Its melting point is low. It is always attached in the circuit in graded form.
- The filaments of electric bulbs is made of **tungsten**. Its melting point is 3110°c.
- Electric fuses are made with metals with low melting point and so that it can melt and break the circuit if electricity flow increases instantly.
- All the instruments are attached in parallel path in the domestic circuit.

Magnet

- Magnet is made of iron and other matters, it attracts iron and when hanged with a cord it always positions itself into the direction of **North and South Pole.**
- The tip that faces the North Pole is called the North Pole of the magnet and the tip that faces the South Pole is called the South Pole of the magnet.
- The same Poles retract while the opposite Poles attract each-other.

Cathode Rays

- Cathode rays were discovered by **Sir William Cook.**

Particle	Mass (KG)	Charge (Coulomb)	Discoverer
Proton	1.672×10^{-27}	$+1.6 \times 10^{-19}$	Eugen Goldstein
Neutron	1.675×10^{-27}	0	James Chadwick
Electron	9.108×10^{-31}	-1.6×10^{-19}	J. J. Thomson

- They travel in a straight line and shine.
- Cathode rays can penetrate though a thin metal sheet.
- Their speed is 1/10th of the speed of light.

Positive or Canal Rays

- Canal Rays were discovered by Eugen Goldstein.
- Canal rays are formed of positively charged particles.
- They travel in straight line and can deposit themselves in magnetic or electrical field.

They ionize the gases

X-Rays

- These are electromagnetic waves, their wave-length range is 0.1A-100A.
- X-rays were discovered by Wilhelm Rontgen.
- X-rays travel in a straight line.
- They are responsible for the occurrence of reflection, refraction, diffraction and polarization etc.
- These rays do not get deposited in the magnetic or electric field. X-rays reflect the light electricity (Photoelectric) effect.

The use of X-Rays

- **In surgery:** X-rays are used to identify broken bones, bullets and stone etc.
- **In radiography:** X-rays are used as the curatives of some diseases. For example, X-rays are used to destroy the cancerous cells.
- **In spying:** these rays can detect hidden objects inside the human body.
- **In engineering:** X-rays are used to detect cracks or bubbles inside the steel beams in the buildings and bridges.
- **In business:** X-rays are used to detect the difference between true and false diamonds and in identifying the pearl inside the oyster.

Radioactivity

- Radioactivity was discovered by **Antoine Henri Becquerel, Marie Curie and Pierre Curie.** These three were awarded joint Nobel Prize for this discovery.
- The nucleus that contains 83 or more protons are unstable. The nuclei start to emit Alpha (α), Beta (β) and Gamma (γ) rays to gain stability. These nuclei are called radioactive.
- Pierre Curie and his wife Marie Curie discovered a new radioactive element – radium.
- All natural radioactive elements turn into glass after emanating α, β and γ rays.

Nuclear Reactor

- Nuclear Reactor is a process by which the energy generated by nuclear diffusion is converted into electrical energy.
- Uranium -235 or Plutonium -239 is used as fuel in the reactor.
- **Cadmium or Boron** Rod is used is controller in the reactor.

Particle	Mass	Charge	Discoverer	Specialty
Positron	9.108×10^{-27}	$+1.6 \times 10^{-19}$	Carl David Anderson	Anti-particle of electron
Neutrino	0	0	Wolfgang Pauli	
Pi-Mason	274 time of electron	Both positive and negative	Yukawa	Unstable, life span is 10^{-8} seconds
Photon	0	0	Einstein	Its motion is equal to the motion of light

The Specialties of α, β and γ Rays

Specialty	α	β	γ
Origin	From nucleus	From nucleus	From nucleus
Nature	Positive	Negative	Neutral
Composition	$_2He^4$	$_1e^0$	Photon
Mass	6.6×10^{-27}kg	9.1×10^{-31}kg	Zero
Charge	+2e	-1.6×10^{-19}C	Zero
Effect on photographic plate	✓	✓	✓
Effect on electric and magnetic field	✓	✓	

CHEMISTRY

Matter

Something that occupies place, has mass and resists any change in its composition is called Matter.

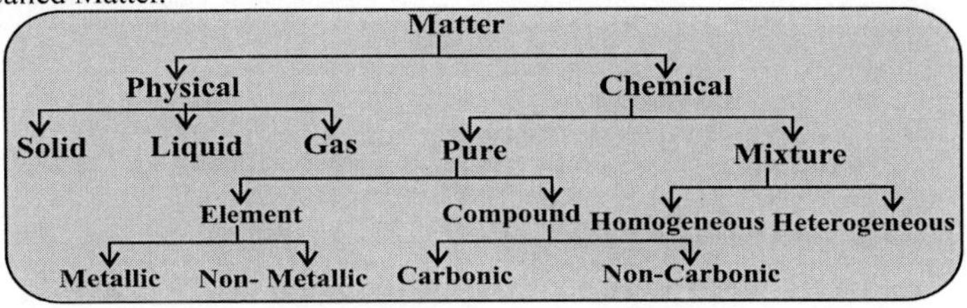

Physical and Chemical Transformations

- The transformations that affect the physical composition of the matter like its color, solidness, density, melting point etc. but does affect its chemical composition chemical properties are called **Physical Transformations.**
- Crystallization, sublimation, boiling, thawing, vaporization, cutting the trees, dissolving of sugar, salt etc. in water are examples of Physical Transformation.
- **Chemical Transformations** affect the chemical composition and chemical properties of the matter, a new matter is formed due to these transformations.
- Burning of fuel, candle, paper, decomposition of water, ripening of fruits etc. are examples of Chemical Transformation.

Boiling Point

Different Techniques of Separating a Mixture

1. Crystallization
2. Distillation
3. Sublimation
4. Fractional Distillation
5. Chromatography
6. Steam Distillation

- The temperature at which the aqueous tension of a liquid becomes equal to the atmospheric pressure is called the **boiling Point** of that liquid.
- **The boiling point increases in the presence of impurities**, hence the boiling point of the oceanic water is higher than that of the pure water.
- As one goes higher in the atmosphere, the atmospheric pressure decreases compared to the sea-level atmospheric pressure.
- Pressure Cooker has higher pressure. This increases the boiling point of the water and the food cooks faster.
- As one goes high up the atmosphere, the atmospheric pressure is less than the air pressure in our lungs. This causes difficulty in breathing.

Melting Point: the temperature at which the solid matter starts to melt into liquid is called the Melting Point of that matter.

Freezing Point: the temperature at which the liquid matter starts to freeze is called the Freezing Point of that matter.

Atom, Molecule and Matter

- Atom is the smallest unit of a matter, it participates in the chemical reactions but it cannot exist in a free state.
- Atoms are made of electrons, protons and neutrons. Protons and neutrons stay in the center (nucleus) of the atom while electron orbits around the center.
- **Molecule** is formed by the combination of atoms. Molecule is the smallest unit of matter that can exist in a free state.
- **The Matter** contains atoms of one type. For example, Carbon (C), Sulphur (S), Diamond, Graphite etc.
- **Isotopes:** these have same number of protons (Atomic Number) whereas the Mass Number (Atomic Number + Number of Neutrons) is variable. Example: H^1, H^2, H^3 etc.
- Isobars: Mass number is constant while Atomic Number varies. Example: $_{18}Ar^{40}$, $_{19}K^{40}$, $_{20}Ca^{40}$ etc.

- Isotone: these have same number of neutrons. For example, ${}_1H^3$ and ${}_2He^4$ have same number of neutrons in their nucleus.
- **Isoelectronic:** The ions and atoms that have same electronic arrangement. For example, **Ne, Na^+, Mg^{++} Al^{+++}** etc.

Pauli's Exclusion Principle: no two electrons in an atom can have identical quantum numbers.

Hund's Rule of Maximum Multiplicity: electrons do not form pairs as long as they have empty space to available, in other words – electrons prefer to stay unpaired.

Heisenberg's Uncertainty Principle: it is impossible to know simultaneously the exact position and momentum of a particle.

Aufbau Principle: the order of writing the increasing energy of atomic brackets in writing the electronic arrangement is as follows:

$1s < 2s < 2p < 3s < 3p < 4s < 3d < 4p < 5s < 4d < 5p < 6s < 4f < 5d < 6p < 7s$

Nuclear Fission

- It is the process by which a heavy nucleus breaks into two or more medium sized nucleus. This process produce immense heat and neutrons.
- Nuclear bomb works on the principle of uncontrolled chain fission. It uses **^{234}Pu** as fuel.

Nuclear Fusion

- Two or more nuclei join to form a heavier nucleus. This process also generates immense heat.
- The Russian scientist **D. I. Mendeleev's** gave a law after the study of elements and their mixtures gave a law. That law is called **Mendeleev's Periodic Law.** The modern periodic table is based on the law of **Henry Moseley**. In his periodic table the elements are arranged columns and rows according to increasing atomic numbers.

Property	Up to Down	Left to Right
Size of atom	Increases	Decreases
Electro +Ve	Increases	Decreases
Ionized energy	Decreases	Increases
Electro -VE	Decreases	Increases
Electron affinity	Decreases	Increases

- **Radiocarbon method is used to determine the age of elements. Uranium Dating is used to determine the age of the earth, minerals and rocks.**

Acid, Base and Salt

- **Acid** are the mixture elements that contain hydrogen as replacement.
- **According to Arrhenius,** acid is a mixture that gives **H^+** ion after dissolving in water.
- According to **Louis Electronic Theory**, acid is a matter that has the tendency to accept the pair of electrons.
- **Aqua Regia:** A mixture in the ratio of 3:1 of concentrated hydrochloric acid and nitric acid. It can melt gold or platinum.

Boyle's Law: For a fixed amount of an ideal gas kept at a fixed temperature, pressure and volume are inversely proportional.

Charles' Law: when the pressure on a sample of a dry gas is held constant, the Kelvin temperature and the volume will be directly proportional.(**$T = 273° + t°C$**)

Avogadro's Law: equal volumes of all gases, at the same temperature and pressure, have the same number of molecules. At normal temperature and pressure, the volume of 1 gram of any gas is 22.4 liters and this 1 liter contains **6.022×10^{23}** molecules.

- This process requires extremely high temperature **(10 K^6)**. That is why this process is also called **Thermonuclear Process.**
- **Hydrogen Bomb and sunlight** are based on Nuclear Fusion.
- In the hydrogen bomb, a nuclear bomb is surrounded with the mixture of Deuterium Oxide **(D_2O)** and Tritium Oxide **(T_2O).**
- **Graham's Rule of Gas Diffusion:**

$$\frac{r_1}{r_1} = \sqrt{\frac{D_2}{D_1}} = \sqrt{\frac{m_2}{m_1}}$$

- **Base:** The mixture that provides salt and water after reacting with acid. According to the theory proposed Bronsted Lowry, the element that is capable of accepting protons is called Base. According to Louis Electronic Theory, the element that has the capacity to donate a pair of electrons is Base.
- **Salt:** Salt and water are produced as a result of the reaction between acid and base.
- **pH Scale:** pH scale is used to measure the acid and base content in a solution.
- **Solution:** Is a homogenous mixture

of two or more matters in which the relative quantities of the soluble and solvent can go under constant change at a certain temperature.

- **Soluble and Solvent:** In a solution the matter that is present in higher quantity is called the Solvent and the matter in low quantity is called Soluble.

Colloid

- Colloid is a heterogeneous solution. It has two phases: Dispersed Phase and Dispersion Medium.

allotropes is called Allotropy.

- **Dispersion:** when the particles of one matter are dispersed around another matter, this process is called Dispersion.
- **Suspension:** in this process the size of the dispersed particles is from $10^{(-3)}$ CM to $10^{(-4)}$ CM or bigger. These particles can be seen from naked eye. These particles are temporary and are prone to deviate from dispersal medium.
- Two main types of carbon are diamond and graphite.

Saturated Solution: A solution made at a certain temperature that has absorbed the maximum possible quantity of the soluble is called a Saturated Solution.

Unsaturated Solution: A solution made at a certain temperature that has the potential of absorbing more soluble at the same temperature is called Unsaturated Solution.

Super Saturated Solution: A Saturated Solution that has the soluble in amount more than what was actually needed to make the solution saturated is called Super Saturated Solution.

- They reflect solution, Tindall Effect (dispersal of light by colloidal particles) and Brownian Speed.
- When Colloidal particles attract toward Dispersion Medium, they are called Liquid Affinitive Colloids. When the Colloidal particles do not show affinity toward Dispersion Medium, they are called Anti-liquid Colloids. Liquid Affinitive Colloids are more stable and reversible.
- Dialysis (a method of colloidal purification) is used in cleaning the blood with the help of liver machine.
- Alum is used for purifying water because it pushes the impurities toward the base of the water.
- **$FeCl_3$** is used in stopping blood leakage because is causes blood clotting.

Carbon and its Compounds

- Allotropy: the matters whose physical properties are different but chemical properties are identical are called 'Allotropes', this event of finding

Brownian Movement: The particles of colloidal solution are always in motion, this motion is called Brownian Movement.

Tyndall Effect: when the light is passed through a colloidal solution and the process is observed through a microscope placed vertically to the solution, one observes the colloidal particles glitter like the tip of the pin against dark background. This is called Tyndall Effect.

Types of Colloid: sol, gel, aerosol, froth, pious

- **Hydrocarbon:** the compound of carbon and hydrogen is called hydrocarbon.
- **Hydrocarbon is of three types:** Saturated Hydrocarbon, Unsaturated Hydrocarbon and Aromatic Hydrocarbon.
- **Isomerism:** The relation of two or more compounds composed of the same kinds and numbers of atoms but differ from each other in structural arrangement. These compounds are called the Isomers of each other. It has two main types: Structural and Cis-trans Isomerism.
- **Polymerization:** The molecules of a compound join and make a bigger molecule. The molecules participating in this process are called Monomers and the final product (bigger molecule) is called a Polymer.
- Two examples of natural Polymers are starch and cellulose.
- **Vulcanization:** The process of mixing natural rubber with Sulphur and heating the mixture is called Vulcanization.

Battery

- Battery is the process that converts chemical energy into electrical energy. Batteries are of two types:
- **Primary Battery:** These cannot be recharged and act like galvanized cell. Example: dry cell, mercury cell etc.
- **Secondary Battery:** These can be recharged and act like both galvanized cell and electrical decomposition cell. Example: glass charging battery, Nickel-

Cadmium battery.

Sources of Energy

- Renewable sources are available in abundance are they shall never deplete. Example: air, sunlight etc.
- Non-Renewable sources are available in a limited quantity and will go deplete after a certain time. Example: minerals, coal, petroleum, natural gas etc.

Fuel

- Fuel are the matters that generate heat and light when burned.
- When 1 gram of a fuel is burned in the excess exposure to air, then the heat it generates is called the Calorific Value of that fuel.
- The fuel used in the rockets is called propellant. Liquid hydrogen and liquid oxygen are used as chief propellants.

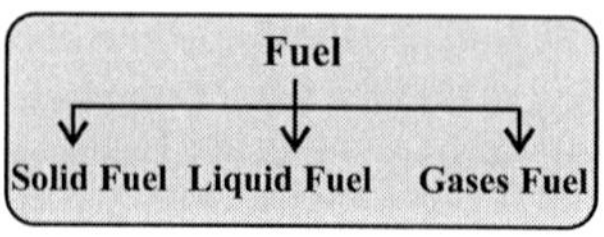

Coal

- Coal is formed by the carbonization of the vegetation. It is found in many forms, e. g. peat coal (60%C), lignite or brown coal (70%C), bituminous coal (80%C) and anthracite coal (90%). Bituminous is the most common type found all around the world.
- **Gaseous Fuel:** natural gas, bio gas, producer gas, water gas, coal gas etc.

Flame

Flame has three parts:

- **Internal Part:** It appears red because of the presence of the unburnt carbon particles. This part has the lowest temperature.
- **Middle Part:** Looks yellow because of the uncomplete burning of the fuel.
- **Outer Part:** Looks blue because of the complete burning of the fuel. This part has the highest temperature. The goldsmiths use this part of the fire to melt gold.

Fire-extinguisher

Water is a good fire-extinguisher. It turns to vapor after coming in the contact of fire. The vapor surround the burning object and blocks its oxygen supply. Thus, fire is extinguished.

Safety Matchstick

A mixture of Antimony Sulfide and potassium chlorate is applied at one end of the safety matchstick and a mixture of crushed glass and red phosphorous is applied on the matchbox.

Metals

- The elements that loose electrons to become positive (except hydrogen) are called metals. Metals are usually shiny, elastic and malleable.
- **Minerals:** the elements or the compounds of elements that are found inside the earth are called minerals.
- **Ore:** the minerals that can be extracted from metals with simple procedure and are useful.
- **Metallurgy:** The various processes of extracting metals out of ores and their purification is called metallurgy.
- **Gangue:** The impure matter extracted from the ore is called gang.

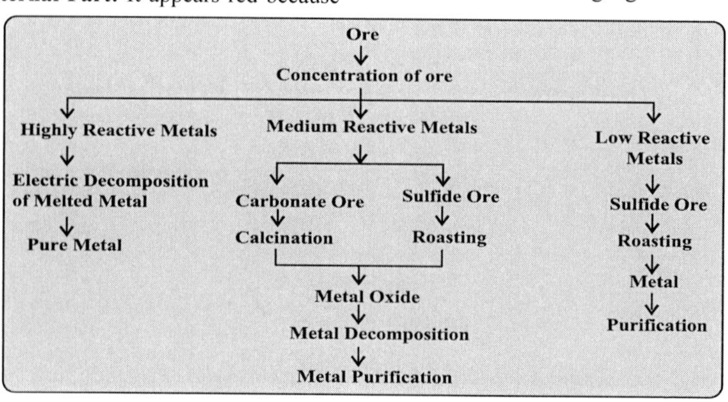

- **Flux:** The matter that is added into the ore to rid it from gangue is called flux.
- **Slang:** The matter that is formed with the mixture of gangue and flux is called slang.
- **Calcination:** in this process the metal ore is heated on the temperature lower than its condensation point to get rid of vaporized impurities.
- **Roasting:** In this process, the metal ore is heated at the temperature lower than its condensation point in the presence of warm air to oxidize the impurities.
- **Smelting:** In this process, the metal is heated at the temperature higher than its condensation point in the presence of coke and flux. This process yields pure metal.

Corrosion

- The wasting of metal surface due to exposure to air and humidity is called Corrosion. It is an electro-chemical process.
- The surface of iron turns brown due to ferric oxide **($Fe_2O_3 . xH_2O$).** This brown surface is called rust.
- Silver turns blackish due to formation of silver sulfide **(Ag_2S)** in the presence of air. Copper's surface turns green due to formation of copper carbonate **$Cu(OH)_2$** . $CuCO_3$.
- Corrosion of iron is called **rusting.**
- Corrosion can be Prevented by electroplating, oil, grease, paint, varnish or galvanization (zinc plating on iron).

Non-metals and Man Made Materials

- Non-metals: modern Periodic Table registers 24 non-metals. 11 of these are gases, 1 is liquid (bromine) and 12 are solid.
- **Cement:** When imestone or chalk is mixed with red sand or rock and the product of this process is cement.
- **Glass:** Glass is a solid mixture of simple glass, silica, sodium silicate and calcium silicate. Glass is a frozen liquid in the form of non-crystal solid. Glass does not have a crystalized form and it does not have a specific melting point.
- **Soap:** All the soaps are the mixture of sodium or potassium salts of high-fat acids. The process of making soaps is called soap-making.
- **Detergent:** It has a long chain of hydrocarbon and a polarized group at the end of the chain. It is better in the sense that its salt is soluble with **Ca^{+2}**, **Mg^{+2}** and **Fe^{+3}**.

Acid and Base

- The matters that turn the blue litmus into red are acids. They usually donate proton into water.
- Base turn the red litmus into blue. Base accept the proton **(H^+)**.

Hard Water

- The water in which bicarbonates of calcium are dissolved is called temporary hard water. In permanent hard water the soluble of calcium and magnesium (I. e. chloride and sulfate) are present.
- Soap does make foam in hard water because of the formation of sulfate chlorite and bicarbonate.
- The temporary hardness of water can be removed by boiling it or adding calcium hydroxide **($Ca(OH)_2$)** into it. This is called Clarke Method.
- To remove the permanent hardness of water, sodium carbonate **(Na_2CO_3)** is added into the water.

Heavy Water

- It is an oxide of heavy hydrogen or deuterium. The molecular weight of heavy water is 20.
- It is used in nuclear reactors.

Hardening of Oil

- When oil (unsaturated fat) is heated with nickel catalyst and hydrogen, it turns into a solid substance, i.e. butter (saturated fat). This process is called Hardening of Oil.

Medicines

Medicines are the chemical substances that are used to cure ailments and alleviation of pain.

Pesticides

Pesticides kill the crop-destroying organisms. There are of following types:

- **Insecticide:** DDT, Gamexane, aluminum
- **Fungicide:** Bordeaux mixture, Organomercury compound
- **Herbicide:** Benzepam, sodium chlorate, sodium arsenate
- **Denticide:** aluminum phosphide
- **Catalysts:** A catalysts is a material that is added to a reaction mixture to accelerate the process but it is itself not participatedis called catalyst and this process is catalysis.

BIOLOGY

Biology is the branch of science concerned with the study of living organisms **(Lamarck and Treviranus, 1802)**. It has three branches: zoology, botany and microbiology. Organisms have been classified into five categories. These categories are: **Monera, Protista, Plantae, Fungi and Animal.** Specie is the basis for this classification.

Some Discoveries Regarding Cells

Scientist	Year	Discovery
Felice Fontana	1781	Nucleoli
Robert Brown	1833	Nucleus
Purkinje	1839	Gave the term Protoplasm
Kolliker	1857	Mitochondria
W. Fleming	1877	Discovered Mitosis
Bender and Bowery	1887	The specie has same number of Chromosomes
Camillo Golgi	1891	Golgi body
C.Benda	1898	Gate the term Mitochondria
W. S. Sutton	1902	Importance of chromosome cell division
Friedrich Meves	1904	Discovery of Plant Mitochondria
J. B. Farmer	1905	Gave the term Amitosis
F. A. Johnson	1909	Formation of Plasma
T. H. Morgan	1933	The role of Chromosomes in Genetics

Cell Science

- The term Protoplasm was given by Purkinje in the year 1839 A. D. this is a thick liquid, colorless, pellucid, ropy and mass containing substance. Protoplasm is responsible for the occurrence of all the biological functions. That is why protoplasm is also called the physical basis of life.
- Two part of protoplasm are Cell Liquid and Nucleus Liquid.
- Two types of Cell: Prokaryotic and Eukaryotic.
- Robert Virchow observed the cell division for the first time in 1855. Cell divisions are mainly of three types: Amitosis, Mitosis and Meiosis.

Mendel's Laws

1. Law of Dominance
2. Law of Segregation
3. Law of Independent Assortment

Genetics

- The transfer of genetic characteristics from generation to generation is called Genetics. Austrian Graham Johann Mendel (1822-1884) first observed Genetics. He is called the Father of Genetics.
- The characteristics of the organism that are observable are called Phenotypes.
- The genetic code of the organism is called Genotype. It is made of genes.

Man Genetics

- W. Walters first gave the name Chromosome in 1888. The genetic substance found in the chromosomes is called Genomes.
- The genes that are found outside the chromosome inside the cell liquid are called Plasma genes.

Organism/ Specie	Chromo somes	Organism/ Specie	Chromo somes
Mosquito	6	House fly	12
Peas	14	Onion	16
Tomato	24	Frog	26
Lemon	18, 36	Cat	38
Mouse	40	Wheat	42
Rabbit	44	Human	46
Potato/Chimpanzee/ Tobacco			48

Parts of Cell

1. Cell wall 2. Cell membrane 3. Centrosome 4. Endoplasmic reticulum 5 ribosome 6. Mitochondria 7. Golgi body 8. Lysosome 9. Plastid (Chloroplast, Leucoplast and Chromoplast) 10. Vacuoles 11. Nucleus

Difference Between DNA and RNA	
DNA	**RNA**
It has deoxyribose sugar	It has ribose sugar
Its base is adenine, guanine, cytosine and thymine	Uracil takes the place of thymine in the base
This is found mainly in the nucleus	This is found both in the nucleus and cell liquid

Organic Evolution

- The evolution of multiple and complex organisms from simple organism is called - **Organic Evolution.**
- **Homologous Organ:** The structures which are similar in their morphology, anatomy, genetics and embryology but dissimilar in their function are called - **Homologous Organs.**
- **Analogous Organ:** The organs which have the same function but different basic structure are called - **Analogous Organs.**
- **Vestigial Organ:** The organs which were fully developed in the ancestors but lost their functional value over time are called **Vestigial Organs.** These organs start to disappear over time.
- **Fossil:** The remains of the organisms which have gone extinct are called **Fossils.** The fossils are found preserved in the rocks near earth's surface. The study of fossils is called **Paleontology.**
- **The branch of biology concerned with the classification of organisms is called Taxonomy.**
- **Carolus Linnaeus** propagated the Binominal **Nomenclature** process of organisms. In this method, the scientific name is made of genus and species of the organism.
- The **modern** process of **nomenclature** is inspired by the process suggested by **Linnaeus.**
- Viruses are miniscule, parasitical, nucleoprotein particles. They get activated inside living organism only. Virus was discovered for the first time in **1892** in tobacco by **Dmitri Ivanovsky.**
- The term Bacteria was given by **Ehrenburg in 1829.**

Botany

- The study of plants and their behavior is called **Botany.**
- **Theophrastus** is considered to be the Father of Botany.
- **Thalophyta is the biggest group of plant world.**
- The study of algae is called **Phycology**.
- **Fungi** is chlorophyll, multinucleate, tissue-less thalophyta. Its cell wall is made of chitin.
- **Bacteria** was discovered by Van **Leeuwenhoek in 1683.** He is also considered the father of **Bacterial Science.**

Plant Morphology

- The study of appearance and characteristics of different parts of plant like - roots, stems, leaves etc. is called **Morphology.**
- **Roots** are the part of plant that grow downwards, they develop from the radicle. Roots are of two type: **Tap Root and Adventitious Root.**
- The flower contains calyx, corolla, androecium and gynoecium. Androecium is male reproductive organ and gynoecium is female reproductive organ.
- **Androecium** has more than one stamens. **The stamens contain pollen grains.**

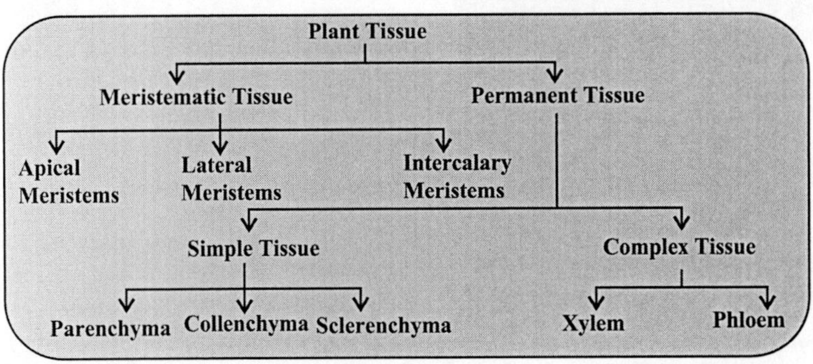

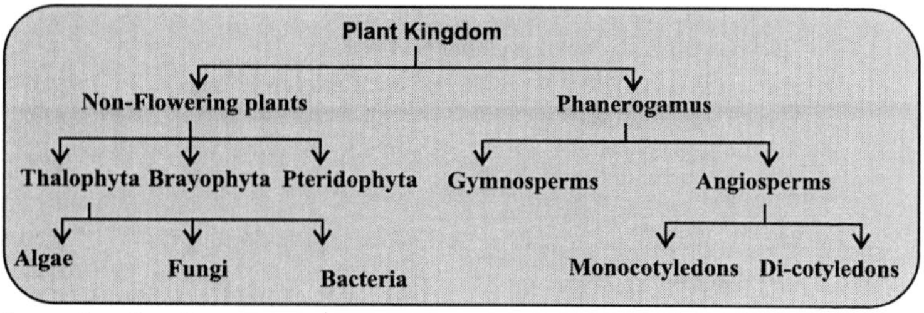

- **Gynoecium** has three parts**: ovary, style and stigma.**
- **Pollination:** the process of transfer of pollens from anther to the edge of style is called Pollination. Pollination is of two types: **Self-Pollination and Cross-Pollination.**
- **Fertilization:** is the process of fusion of the female gamete, the ovum or egg, and produced by the pollen grain in the pollen tube. The fertilized egg is called **Zygote.**
- All the fruits have been categorized into three categories: Simple fruits, Aggregate fruits and Composite fruits.
- **Calyx and corolla** take part in the formation of some fruits. These fruits are called **False Fruits.** Example: apple, jack fruit.
- The group of cells with similar origin, structure and functions is called a **Tissue.**

Photosynthesis

- The process by which green plants and some other organisms use sunlight to synthesize nutrients from carbon dioxide and water.

$$6CO_2 + 12H_2O \xrightarrow[\text{Chlorophyll}]{\text{sunlight}} \underset{\text{Glucose}}{C_6H_{12}O_6} + \underset{\text{Water}}{6H_2O} + \underset{\text{Oxygen}}{6O_2}$$

- **Chlorophyll** contains an atom of magnesium in its nucleus.
- Chlorophyll absorbs **violet, blue and red** color from the sunlight.
- Photosynthesis has two stages: **photo chemical and dark chemical.**
- Plant hormones: 1. Auxins 2. Gibberellins 3. Cytokinins 4. Abscisic Acid or ABA 5. Ethylene 6. Florigens 7. Traumatin

Human Anatomy

The functional and structural unit of human body is Cell. Similar cells unite to form Tissues. Tissues unite to form organs and organs unite to form organ-system. Some of the organ-systems in the human body are – digestive system, respiratory circulation, nervous system and endocrine system.

Nutrition

- Carbohydrates, vitamins, protein etc. are nutrients.
- The food that contains all the nutrients in balanced is called **Balanced Diet**.
- 70-80% of human life is made of water.

Respiration

Respiration is an oxidization and energy-providing process. In this process, complex carbonic compounds are broken into simple carbonic compounds.

Blood

- Blood is a thin, acidic (pH 7.4), opaque, slimy liquid made of plasma and blood cells.
- **Plasma:** contains 90-92% water, 1-2% non-carbonic salt, 6-7% plasma protein and 1-2% carbonic compounds.
- **The Red Blood Cells** are oval shaped, bi-convex and nucleic in all the vertebrates except mammals.
- **RBCs** contain respiratory pigment – **Hemoglobin**. It transports the oxygen inside the body.
- **White Blood** Cells are nucleic, pigment-less cells. They protect the body from viruses.
- **Blood Platelets** are colorless and do not have a nucleus. They play an important part in blood clotting.

Circulatory System

- **Open Circulatory** System is found in cockroaches, prone, insects and spider etc.
- **Closed Circulatory** System is found in Annelida, mollusk and all the vertebrates.
- **Heart** is a **big,** muscle constricting, **self-pumping organ.**
- **Fish** have two-chambered, amphibians and reptiles have three-chambered and birds and mammals have four-chambered heart.
- The **normal blood pressure** of an **animal** is **120-80 mmHg.**

- The heartbeat rate of newborn baby is close to **140 beats** per minute.
- Prothrombin, fibrinogen, **Ca^{+2}** and **vitamin K** participate in blood clotting.

Execratory System

- Different animals execrate different types of nitrogen waste.
- The main execratory organ in the human body is **kidney**. This is made of small functional and structural units called **Nephron.**

Nervous System

- This consists of Central, Peripheral and Autonomic Nervous Systems.
- Central Nervous System consists of brain and spinal cord.
- Brain is divided into **three** parts: Prosencephalon (fore-brain), Mesencephalon (middle brain) and Rhombencephalon (back brain).

Skeletal System

Human skeletal system is formed of two parts

1. Axial Skeleton: skull, vertebral column
2. Appendicular Skeleton: girdles, pedal bones

Human Anatomy

Fact	**Location/ Quantity**
Total number of bone	206
The smallest bone	Stapes (in the ear)
The longest bone	Femur (in the thigh)
The number of vertebrae	33
The number of muscles	639
The longest muscle	Sartorius muscle
The length of the large Intestine	1.5 M
The length of the Small Intestine	6.25 M
The weight of the liver (in males)	1.4 – 1.8 KG
The wgt. of the liver (in females)	1.2 – 1.4 KG
The largest gland	Liver
The organ with maximum regeneration capacity	Liver
The organ with minimum regeneration capacity	Brain
The strongest part of the body	Tooth enamel
The longest salivation gland	Parotid gland
The normal temperature of the body	98.4° F (37° C)
The amount of blood in the body	5.5 liter
The average amount of hemo-globin (in males)	13.16g/dl
The average amount of hemo-globin (in females)	11.5-14g/dl
The number of WBCs	5000-10000/ cu mm
The smallest WBC	Lymphocyte
The biggest WBC	Monocyte
The life-span of WBCs	120 days
The life-span of RBCs	2-5 days
The time taken in blood clotting	3-6 minutes
Universal Recipient blood group	AB
Universal Donor blood group	O
Average blood pressure	120/80 Hg
Heartbeat rate in adults	72 times per minute
The biggest artery	Abdominal aorta
The weight of kidney	150 gram
The weight of brain	1220-1400 grams
The length of spinal cord	42-45 C.M
The number of cranial nerves	12 pairs
The number of spinal nerves	31 pairs
The longest nerve	Sciatic
The thinnest and smallest nerve	Treaclier
The biggest nerve	Trigeminal
The biggest cell	Nerve cells
The biggest endocrine gland	Thyroid

Some Important Facts Regarding Zoology

Specialty	Name
The biggest mammal	Blue whale
The biggest land-dwelling mammal	Elephant
The biggest bone	Femur
The biggest vein	Inferior vena cava
The biggest land bird	Ostrich
The biggest reptile	Turtle
The most venomous snake in the world	Australian Peninsular Tiger Snake
The smallest sparrow	Hummingbird
Toothless mammal	Ant Eater
The busiest organ of the body	Liver
The heaviest organ of the body	Liver
The heaviest vertebrate	Lumber
The strongest muscle	The jaw muscle
Calories needed in a day (males)	3900 Kilocalories
Calories needed in a day (females)	2400 Kilocalories
The oldest primate	Lemur
The oldest arthropod	Parapets
The oldest mammal	Echidna
The oldest ape	Gibbon
The most venomous Indian snake	King Cobra

Vitamins: Sources, Functions and Deficiency Effect			
Name	Source	Biological Effects	Deficiency Effects
Vitamin – A (Retinol)	Milk, butter, egg, liver and fish oil	Color synthesis, growth and development of epithelium levels	Night-blindness, xerophthalmia, cell-scales, stunted growth, dryness disease, Osteomalacia
Vitamin – D (Calciferol)	Butter, liver, fish oil, lungs, egg, skin and photo - synthesis in yeast	Metabolic of calcium and phosphorus, growth of bones and teeth	Dryness disease, osteomalacia
Vitamin – E (Tocopherol)	Oil, wheat, the yolk of the egg, soybean	Cell protection, growth of birth epithelium, muscle activation	Decline in birth capacity, weakness in reproductive organ and muscles
Vitamin – K (Naphthoquinone)	Green leaves, egg, liver, tomato, cauliflower,soy-bean, intestinal bacteria	Synthesis of prothrombin in the liver	Deficient blood clotting leading to blood loss
Water Soluble Vitamins			
Vitamin – B_1 (Thymine)	Cereal, legume, soybean milk, yeast, egg, meat	Necessary metabolic for carbohydrate and amino acid, co-enzyme of enzymes	Beriberi
Vitamin – B_2 (Riboflavin)	Cheese, egg, yeast, green leaves, meat and liver	Element of metabolically important co-enzymes FAD and FMN	Cheilosis
Vitamin – B_3 (Nicotinic Acid)	Yeast, meat, liver, fish, egg, milk, peas, dry fruitsand legume	Element of metabolically important co-enzymes NAD and NAPD	Pellagra
Vitamin – B_5 (Pantothenic Acid)	Egg, liver, meat, milk, tomato, groundnut and sugarcane	Element of catabolism of co-enzyme A	Skin diseases, stunted growth, whitening of hair and decreased reproductive capacity
Vitamin – B_6 (Pyridoxine)	Milk, yeast, cereal, meat, liver and fish	Co-enzyme of the enzymes important in protein metabolism	Blood deficiency, skin diseases and muscle contortion
Vitamin – K	Meat, wheat, egg, fruits groundnut, chocolate, vegetables, and yeast	Co-enzyme in synthesis reactions of many materials	Skin diseases, hair-fall
Folic Acid group	Green leaves, Soyabean, liver, yeast, legume and intestinal bacteria	Growth, formation of blood particles, DNA synthesis	Blood deficiency, stunted growth
Vitamin – B_{12}	Meat, fish, liver, egg, milk, intestinal bacteria	Growth, formation of blood particles, synthesis of nucleic acids	Blood deficiency, nervous system diseases
Vitamin – C	Fruits of the lemon family, tomato, potato vegetables, and other fruits	Inter-cellular cement, formation of collagen, bone matrix and teeth dentine	Scurvy

Medical Instruments			
Pacemaker	Heartbeat rate	Electroencephalograph	Brain
Auto-Analyzer	Glucose, cholesterol level detection, urea	Computed Tomography Scan (CT Scan)	Full body
		Electrocardiograph	Heart

Diseases Caused by Bacteria in Humans			
Disease	**Affected Organ**	**Symptoms**	**Bacteria**
Pneumonia	Lungs	Lung infection, pulmonary edema, high fever, difficulty in breathing	Diplococcus pneumoniae
Botulism	Nervous system	Vomiting, double vision	Clostridium botulinum
Leprosy	Skin and nerves	Boils and tumor formation, gradual decaying of hand and feet tissues	Mycobacterium leproae
Tuberculosis	Any part of body especially lungs	Fever, cough, weakness, breathing difficulty, phlegm and blood in saliva	Mycobacterium tuberculosis
Cholera	Intestine	Dehydration, vomiting	Vibrio comma
Diphtheria	Trachea (wind pipe)	High fever, breathing difficulty, choking	Corynebacterium diphtherae
Whooping cough	Respiratory system	Relentless cough, vomiting with cough	Hemophilus pertussis
Plague	Armpits, lungs, RBCs	High fever, swollen lymph glands, fainting	Treponemapestis
Meningitis	Upper membranes of the brain	High fever, fainting, swelling in the brain membranes	Neisseria meningitides
Tetanus	Nerves and muscles	Fainting, lockjaw, jerking of the body	Clostridium tetani
Periodic fever	Intestine	Fever weakness, holes in the intestine during high fever	Salmonella typhi or Eberthella typhosa
Syphilis	Reproductive organ, brain, nervous system	Formation of spots on the reproductive organ, paralysis, grains on the skin, hair-fall pallidum	Treponema

Diseases Caused by Protozoa in Humans			
Disease	Affected Organ	Symptoms	Parasite
Pyorrhea	Teeth-roots and gums	Gum-swelling, blood leakage and pus leakage	Entamoeba gingivalis
Loose-Motion	Large intestine	Swelling and pain in the large intestine, chronic loose-motion	Trichomonas Hominis
Amoebiasis	Large intestine (cologne)	Swelling in the cologne, mucus leakage with loose-motion	Entamoeba histolytica
Dysentery	The initial portions of the intestine	Loose-motion, headache and sometimes causes jaundice	Giardia lamblia
Gonorrhea (in males) and White Discharge (in females)	Urinal tract in males and vagina in females	Burning and pain in urination, discharge of white liquid in women and pain	Trichomonas vaginalis
Loose Motion (Isosporiasis)	Small intestine, blood, bone-marrow, spleen	Contortion in Small Intestine and loose motion	Isospora hominis
Epidemic Encephalitis	Blood, cerebro-spinal liquid and central nervous system	High fever, fainting, long sleep	Trypanosoma gambiens
Malaria	Red blood particles, spleen and kidney	High fever, headache, back ache	Plasmodium malariae

Diseases Caused by Fungus

Disease	Affected Organs	Responsible Fungus
Aspergillus Fumigatus	Ears and lungs	Aspergillus Flavus, A. fumigatus
Boils	Throat & mouth	A.Niger and monilia
Cryptococcal disease	Nervous system	Crypotococcus neoformans
Pollen fever	Whole body	Alternaria,and Trichoderma specie
Tetter	Skin	Microsporum lenosun

Diseases Caused by Viruses in Humans

Disease	Affected organs
Tonsil	Parotid saliva glands
Trachoma	Eyes
Dengue	Muscles and joints
Flu or Influenza	Respiratory system
Rabies or hydrophobia	Nervous system
Small-pox	Whole body, especially feet and hands
Jaundice (enters the body via food and water)	Nervous system (destroys the motor nerves of spinal cord)
Herpes	Skin, mucous-membrane
Encephalitis or brain Swelling	Nervous system

Material	**Bacteria**
Butter Milk	Lactobacillus vulgaricus
Yoghurt	Lactobacillus thermophillus
Curd	Streptococcus lactis
Cheese	Lactobacillus and Streptococcus cremoris
Acetone - Butanol	Clostridium acetobutylicum
Lactic acid	Lactobacillus delbrueckii and Rhizopus oryzae
Lysine	Micrococcus glutamicus
Insulin and interferon	Recombinant and variety of E.coli
Streptokinase	Streptococcus equisimilis
Citric acid	Aspergillus niger
Fumaric acid	Rhizopus nigricans
Gibberellic acid	Furesium Moniliform
Zymes	Saccharomyces species
Pectinus	Aspergillus venti
Beer, rum, scotch, alcohol	Saccharomyces species

Diseases and the Organs Affected by Them

Disease	**Affected Organs**
Arthritis	Joint swelling
Diphtheria	Throat, wind pipe
Echzema	Skin
Jaundice	Kidney
Pleurisy	Chest
Pyorrhea	Teeth and gums
Rheumatism	Joints
Tetanus	Nervous system, muscles
Leprosy	Skin, nerves
Cholera	Intestine, food canal
Whooping cough	Respiratory system
Cataract, glaucoma	Eyes
Tetter	Skin
Cryptococcal disease	Nervous system
Hepatitis - B	Liver
Trachoma	Kidney, eyes and pancreatitis
Diabetes	Pancreatitis, kidney and eyes
Goiter	Thyroid gland
Parkinson	Brain
Pneumonia	Lungs
Typhoid	Intestine
Rickets	Bones
Syphilis	Reproductive organ
Loose-motion	Large intestine
Diarrhea	Starting point of the intestine
Gonorrhea and White Discharge	Urinary tract
Isosporiasis	Blood, bones and spleen
Athlete foot	Feet
Boils	Throat and mouth
Meningitis	Spinal cord and brain

Important Antibiotics, their Source and Functions

Antibiotic	Name of the Microbe	Function
Penicillin	Penicillium notatum	Tonsillitis, prevention from rheumatism fever
Griseofulivin	Penicillium griseofulivin	Prevention from tetter
Streptomycin	Streptomycin griseofulivin	Prevention from T.B, meningitis, pneumonia
Chloramphen-icol	Streptomyces venezuelei	Prevention from typhoid and intestinal infection
Tetracycline	Streptomyces aureofaciens	Prevention from viral, pneumonia, whooping cough and eye infection
Terramycin	Streptomyces rimosus	Prevention from viral, typhoid and intestinal infection
Erythromycin	Streptomyces erithrius	Prevention from whooping cough and diphtheria
Bacitracin	Bacillus licheniformus	Prevention from reticulitis lymphonima

Medicinal Plants

Normal Name	Botanical Name	Family	Main Part of the Plant
Sarpgandha	Rauvolfia Serpentina	Apocynaceae	Roots
Opium poppy	Papaver Somniferum	Papaveraceae	Capsule fruit
Belladonna	Atropa Belladonna	Solanaceae	Dry leaves and roots
Datura	Datura Stramonium	Solanaceae	Fruits and juice
Amla	Emblica Officinalis	Euphorbiaceae	Fruits
Strychnine	Strychnon nux-vomica	Loganiaceae	Seeds

Important Facts about Botany

Specialty	Name
The smallest virus	Parvovirus (18-26 nm)
The biggest virus	TMV (300 nm)
Parasite	Pox (280 nm)
The smallest bacteria	Dialister (2 m)
The biggest bacteria	Beggiatoa Mirabilis
The smallest bryophyte	Jupcis
The biggest bryophyte	Dawsonia
The biggest pterido-phyte	Cyathea
The smallest gymno-sperm	Zamia Pygmaea
The biggest gymno-sperm	Sequoia Gigantea
The smallest angio-sperm	Wolffia
The biggest angiosperm	Eucalyptus Regnans
The smallest flower	Rafflesia Arnoldii
The biggest flower	Orchid
The broadest leaf	Victoria Regia
The heaviest wood	Guaiacum Officinale
The biggest unicellular plant	Acetabularia
The amphibians of the plant world	Bryophyte
Vascular Cryptogams	Pteridophyte
Walking fern	Adiantum
Maidenhair fern	Adiantum
Maidenhair tree	Ginkgo Biloba
Most protein-rich algae	Spirulina

Fruits and their Edible Parts

Fruit	Part
Papaya	Middle membrane
Coconut	Embryo sac
Tomato	Ovule and fruit membrane
Apple	Torus
Pear	Torus
Mango	Middle membrane
Banana	Middle and internal mem-brane
Guava	Ovule and fruit membrane
Grape	Ovule and fruit membrane
Orange	juicy fibers
Jack fruit	Perianth and seeds
Groundnut	Cotyledon and embryo
Wheat	Embryo sac and embryo
Cashew	Cotyledon and pedicel
Grams	Cotyledon and embryo
Litchi	Aril
Mulberry	Juicy perianth
Pineapple	Perianth/perigone

- Oxygen was not present at the planet when life first appeared here.
- Bones are strong as concrete and solid like granite.
- Almost 150 lakh cells get destroyed in the body every second.
- Kidney weighs almost 140 grams.
- Human body has almost 50 lakh hairs.

COMPUTER

- Computer is an – **Electronic Machine**
- The father of modern computer – **Charles Babbage (Mathematician)**
- Who discovered abacus– **The Chinese**
- Who discovered the calculator in 1642 – **Pascal (French)**
- The correct order in which popular company Apple released them is – **Mac, iPod, iPhone, iPad**
- "Macintosh" an Operating System is a product of – **Apple**
- Who discovered the first electronic computer (1946) – **J. P. Eckert**
- The first electronic computer was called – **ENIAC**
- Who discovered the IBM PC in 1981 – **William C. Law**
- When was the first Analytical Engine invented – **In 1833**
- A computer store the results for future use – **In the memory**
- The memory is located in – **The CPU**
- The full form of CPU is – **Central Processing Unit**
- How many types does memory have – **2**
- Primary Memory is of – **2 types**
- The small, shiny arrow on the computer screen is called – **cursor**
- Secondary memory is of – **3 types**
- The full form of RAM – **Random Access Memory**
- The full form of ROM – **Read Only Memory**
- The number of buttons in the Computer Keyboard – **101**
- The process of shutting a computer down is called – **Shut Down**
- The process of starting a computer is called – **Boot-up**
- The brain of the computer – **CPU**
- Monitor is called – **VDU**
- The number of Function Keys in the Computer keyboard – **12**
- The full form of MICR – **Magnetic Character Ink Recognization**
- The process of converting Analog Signal into Digital Signal is called – **Digitalization**
- The first computer made in India – **Siddharth**
- The chip connecting points on the Mother Board are called – **Sockets**
- The magnetic disk is coated with – **Iron Oxide**
- Binary Number System uses– **0 and 1**
- 1 KB is equal to – **1024 Bytes**
- The first general purpose computer knowns as – **UNIVAC**
- Norton is – **Anti-Virus tool**
- Virus is – **A program**
- The IC chip of the computer is made of – **Silicon**
- The full form of WWW is – **World Wide Web**
- WWW was discovered in the years – **1989-90**
- WWE is – **An Internet Service**
- John Napier invented the Mini-Computer in the year – **1614**
- Hard Disk is – **Secondary memory**
- World's biggest computer network is – **Internet**
- What is used to align the speed of CPU and Main Memory – **Cache Memory**
- The full form of CD-ROM – **Compact Disc Read Only Memory**
- Disconnecting the network communication is called – **Log out**
- Full form of LAN – **Local Area Network**

Founder of Social Sites

* **Twitter:** Biz Stone, Evan Williams, Noah Glass, Jack Dorsey
* **Facebook:** Chris Hughes, Dustin Moskovitz, Eduardo Saverin, Mark Zuckerberg
* **Google:** Larry Page, Sergey Brin
* **Youtube:** Jawed Karim, Chad Hurley, Steve Chen

- The processing speed of the computer is measured by – **Megahertz**
- Full form of WAN – **Wide Area Network**
- India's first supercomputer is – **PARAM Padma**
- The term PARAM is related to – **computer**
- Pacman computer Program was built for – **playing games**
- The mechanic parts of the computer are called – **hardware**
- The full form of DOS – **Disc Operating System**
- Computer functions mathematical equations with the process – **Registers**
- The process of keeping the data safe – **Backup Plan**
- Virus is – **Destructive program**
- The extension of MS Word – **.doc**
- The full form of FAT – **File Allocation Table**
- The maximum number of columns and rows in the Work Sheet – **1024 and 1025 respectively**
- The unit of speed of the Line Printer – **Line per minute**
- Vacuum Tube used – **In the computers of first generation**
- The full form of MAN – **Metropolitan Area Network**
- The message sent on the internet is called – **E-mail**
- Who made the Power Point – **Microsoft**
- An error in a Computer Programe or Computer hardware is called – **Bug**
- Source Program is – **The transformation of high level language program into Machine Language**
- The speed of Hard Disc is – **3600 rounds per minute**
- The full form of HTTP – **Hyper Text Transfer Protocol**
- The rotation speed of the Floppy Disc – **150-250 rounds per minute**
- The full form of HTML – **Hyper Text Markup Language**
- COBOL Language is used in – **business**
- The home page of the computer is called – **Desktop**
- Joystick is used for – **Playing games**
- The full form of PC – **Personal Computer**
- Computer Data is called – **Information**
- The first calculating device was – **Abacus**
- The full form of ALU – **Arithmetic Logical Unit**
- Mouse, Key Board, Joystick and Light Pen are – **Input Device**
- The full form of IBM – **International Business Machine**
- The unit for measuring the speed of Hard Disc – **R.P.M**
- The first Computer Language was – **FORTRAN**
- Compiler is used for – **Converting High Level language into Machine Language**
- Dos and Windows are – **Operating System**
- The file name can contain maximum – **8 characters**
- How many characters are there in the File Extension – **3 characters**
- LOTUS is – **Computer Software**
- Y2K problem is related to –**Computer**
- 1 Byte contains – **8 Bits**
- Who developed the computer PARAM - 1000 – **C-DAC**
- The assembly language of computer is – **binary digits**
- Floppy is – **A memory device**
- The computer that performs mathematical calculations – **Digital Computer**
- Who developed integrated Circuit Chip – **J. S. Kilby**
- The smallest unit of computer data is –**Bit**
- The computer of the fourth generation is – **Microprocessor**
- How many generations of the computer have been developed – **5**
- The modern computer was developed in – **1946**
- The world's fastest is – **Tianhe-2**
- The name of the first electronic digital computer Suptercomputer – **ENIAC**
- Computer Education Day is celebrated on – **2nd, December**
- The first computerized post office of India is located in – **New Delhi**

Miscellaneous

Some Major Countries of the World, their Capitals and currency

Country	Capital	Currency
India	New Delhi	Rupees
Pakistan	Islamabad	Rupees
Nepal	Kathmandu	Rupees
Sri Lanka	Colombo	Rupees
Bangladesh	Dhaka	Taka
Bhutan	Thimphu	Ngultrum
Myanmar	Yangon	Kyat
Afghanistan	Kabul	Afghani
Maldives	Male	Rupees
China	Beijing	Yuan
Japan	Tokyo	Yen
Thailand	Bangkok	Thai Bhat
Vietnam	Hanoi	Dang
North Korea	Pyongyang	Won
South Korea	Seoul	Won
Singapore	Singapore	Singapore Dollar
Indonesia	Jakarta	Rupees
United Arab Emirates	Abu Dhabi	Dirham
Saudi Arabia	Riyadh	Saudi Riyal
Syria	Damascus	Syrian Pound
Egypt	Cairo	Pound
South Africa	Pretoria	Rand
Libya	Tripoli	Dinar
Congo	Kinshasa	Congo Frank
Greece	Athens	Euro
Belgium	Brussels	Euro
Denmark	Copenhagen	Crone
France	Paris	Euro
Spain	Madrid	Euro
Portugal	Lisbon	Euro
Italy	Rome	Euro
Bulgaria	Sophia	Leva
Great Britain	London	Pound Sterling
Russia	Moscow	Ruble
Poland	Warsaw	Zloty
Hungary	Budapest	Forint
Norway	Oslo	Krone
Germany	Berlin	Euro
Finland	Helsinki	Euro
Netherland	Amsterdam	Euro
Czech Republic	Prague	Czech Koruna
Switzerland	Berne	Frank
Ukraine	Kiev	Hryvnia
Ireland	Dublin	Euro
United States of America	Washington D.C	Dollar
Canada	Ottawa	Dollar
Argentina	Buenos Aires	Peso
Brazil	Rio de Janeiro	Real
Australia	Canberra	Dollar
Fiji	Suva	Dollar
New Zealand	Wellington	Dollsar

The Biggest, Longest, Highest and Smallest in the World

Biggest continent **- Asia**

Smallest continent **- Australia**

Biggest country (area-wise) **- Russia**

Biggest temple **-Angkor Wat temple(Combodia)**

Biggest waterfall **- Angel (Venezuela)**

Highest volcano **- Mount Cotopaxi, Ecuador**

Biggest volcano **- Mauna Loa (Hawaii Islands)**

Longest mountain range **- Andes (S. America)**

Biggest and deepest ocean **- Pacific ocean**

Country with longest border **- Canada**

Country with smallest border **- Gibraltar**

The country with maximum neighbors **- Russia and China (14 neighbors each)**

Longest railway line **- Trans-Siberian Railway (length 9438 KM)**

Biggest zoo **- Etosha Reserve, Namibia**

Highest airport **- Lhasa Gonggar Airport (Tibet)**

Longest river **- Nile**

Widest river **- Amazon**

Biggest salt water lake **- Caspian sea**

Biggest sweet water lake **-Superior(USA)**

Deepest lake **- Lake Baikal, Siberia**

Biggest desert **- Sahara deserts**

Biggest highway **-Trans-Canadian highway (Saint Jones to Vancouver)**

Biggest railway tunnel **-Simplon 2 Tunnel (Switzerland)**

Biggest river dam **-Hirakund Dam (Mahanadi, India)**

Biggest swamp **-Pantanal swamp**

Highest mountain peak **-Mount Everest, height – 8848 meters (Nepal, Himalaya)**

Biggest island **- Indonesia**

City with highest population **- Shanghai**

Biggest bay **- Bay of Mexico**

Highest plateau **- Tibetan plateau**

Biggest railway platform -Gorakhpur(U.P)
Biggest railway station - **Grand Central Terminal, New York**
Biggest delta - **Sundarvan**
Highest waterfall - **Salto Angels fall**
Biggest park - **Yellowstone**
Biggest sundial - **Samrat Yantra, Jaipur**
Smallest river - **D River (USA)**
Smallest country - **Vatican City**
Highest road - **Leh-Manali road**
Highest minar - **Qutb Minar**
Biggest planetarium -**Miyazaki(Japan)**
Highest animal - **Giraffe**
Biggest bird - **Ostrich**
Smallest bird - **Hummingbird**
Smartest animal - **Chimpanzee**
The longest wall - **The Great Wall of China**
Biggest stadium -**Strahov Stadium, Prague**
Biggest indoor stadium - **Superdome Louisiana (USA)**
Place with highest rainfall - **Mawsinram, Meghalaya (India)**
Biggest port - **New York (USA)**
Biggest museum - **British museum, London**
Biggest library -**Congress Library, London**
Biggest epic - **Mahabharata**
Biggest peninsula -**Arabic peninsula**
Biggest river island - **Majuli island, Brahmaputra (Assam)**
Biggest influx - **The influx of Ob river, Russia**
Biggest canal - **Suez canal**
Busiest canal - **Kiel canal**
Highest lake (navigation) - **Titicaca Lake (S.Africa)**
Biggest lagoon - **Lagoa das Patas, Brazil**
Widest waterfall -**Khone Phapheng Falls (Laos)**
Biggest strait -**Davis strait (Greenland and Baffin Island)**

Some Important Countries and Their Political Parties

India Indian National Congress, Bhartiya Janta Party, Aam Aadmi Party, Communist Party of India

Pakistan Muslim League, Pakistan People's Party, Tehrik-i-Pakistan

USA Democratic Party, Republican Party

England Labor Party, Conservative Party, Liberal Democratic Party

Iraq Bath Party

France Socialist Party, National Front, Union for French Democracy

China Communist Party of China

Australia Labor Party, Liberal Party

Bangladesh Bangladesh Nationalist Party, Abami League

Sri Lanka United National Party, Freedom Party

South Africa African National League, National Party, Inkatha Freedom Party

Russia Communist Party, Liberal Democratic Party, Choice Freedom

Some Important Countries and Their Parliaments

Country	Name of the Parliament
India	Sansad (Rajya Sabha and Lok Sabha)
Egypt	People's Assembly
Poland	Sejm
Pakistan	National Assembly
France	National Assembly and Senate
Russia	Duma
South Africa	Parliament (National Assembly and Senate)
Spain	Crotes
Maldives/Iran	Majlis
Nepal	Rashtriya Panchayat
China	National People's Council
Germany	Bundestag
USA	Congress (House of Representative and Senate)
Iraq	National Assembly
Turkey	Grand National Assembly
Afghanistan	Shora
Britain	Parliament
Denmark	Folketing
Canada	Parliament
Bangladesh	Jatiya Sansad

Energy Conversion Instruments

Dynamo Converts mechanical energy into electric energy

Candle Converts chemical energy into light and heat

Microphone Sound energy into electric energy

Loudspeaker Electric energy into sound energy

Solar cell Solar energy into electric energy

Countries and their National Emblems

India	Ashoka Chakra	**Australia**	Vettel
Bangladesh	Water lily	**Canada**	Mapleleaf
Netherland	Lion	**Turkey**	Moon & star
U.K	White lily	**Norway**	Lion
Italy	White lily	**Japan**	Chrysanthemum
Iran	Rose	**USA**	Bald eagle
Spain	Coat of Arms of Spain		
France	Lily		

Important New-Papers of the World

Dawn	Karachi	**Pravda**	Moscow
The Island	Colombo	**Eastern Sun**	Singapore
Al-Ahram	Cairo	**Mainichi Shimbun**	Tokyo
Merkeda	Jakarta	**People's Daily**	Beijing
La Repubblica	Rome	**Le Monde**	Paris
Guardian, Daily Mail	London		
Daily Mirror	London	**The Hindu**	India
The Indian Express	India		
New York Times	New York		
Daily News	New York		

The First in India

International telegraph Service	Mumbai to London (1851)
Wire line	Diamond harbor to Calcutta (1853)
Football club	Mohan Bagan (1899)
Hydroelectric project	Shivasamudram, 1902
New paper	Bengal Gazette (James Hickey)
Vernacular news daily	Samachar Darpan
Hindi news paper	Udanta Martand
Television center	New Delhi (1959)
Silent film	Raja Harishchandra
Talky film	Alamara
Satellite	Aryabhatta (19th April, 1975)
India-made satellite	Inset-2 A (1992)
Atomic test	Pokhran (18th May, 1978)
Test-tube baby	Baby Harsha (1986)
India-made missile	Prithvi (1988)
Coal mine	Raniganj (West Bengal)
Aircraft carrier warship	INS Vikrant
India-made atomic submarine	INS Chakra

Countries and Their National Monuments

Monument	**Location**	**Country**
Taj Mahal	Agra	India
Statue of Liberty	New York	USA
The Hanging Tower	Pisa	Italy
Pyramids	Giza	Egypt
Cremlin	Moscow	Russia
Imperial Palace	Tokyo	Japan
Opera House	Sidney	Australia
Eiffel Tower	Paris	France
Great Wall	Northern China	China

Important News Agencies Around the World

Agency	Country
P.T.I (BHASHA in Hindi)	India
Hindustan Samachar	India
U.N.I (VARTA in Hindi)	India
India News Service (I.N.S)	India
Xinhua	China
Reuter's	Britain
Agency for Press (A.F.P)	France
Unites Press of America	USA
Associated Press (A.P)	USA
Tass	Russia
Antara	Indonesia

Cultural Institutions of India

Institution	**Year of Establishment**
Indian Archaeological Survey	1861
Indian National Archives	1881
Central Secretariat Library	1891
Indian Human Science Survey	1945
National Library (Kolkata)	1948
Sangeet Natak Academy	1953
Indira Gandhi National Art Center	1954
Lalit Kala Academy	1954
National School of Drama	1959

Biggest, Longest, Smallest and Highest in India

The highest minar	Qutb Minar (Delhi)
Biggest road bridge	M. Gandhi bridge (Patna)
Biggest animal fair	Sonpur (Bihar)
Highest mountain peak	Godwin Austin (K-2)
Highest dam	Bhakhra Nangal dam (Punjab)
Biggest desert	Thar (Rajasthan)
Biggest cave temple	Kailash temple (Elora)
Biggest zoo	Zoological Garden
Biggest tunnel	Jawahar Tunnel
Biggest delta	Sundarban (West Bengal)
State with highest forest density	M.P.
Biggest corridor	Rameshvaram (Tamilnadu)
Highest waterfall	Jog or Garsopa (Karnataka)
Biggest dome	Gol Gumbad (Bijapur)
Highest idol	Gomteshvar (Karnataka)
Place with highest rainfall	Mawsinram, Meghalaya
Biggest liver bridge	Howrah Bridge (Kolkata)
Biggest canal	Indira Gandhi canal
Biggest railway platform	Gorakhpur, U. P.
Biggest stadium	Yuva Bharti, Salt Lake
Biggest sun temple	Konark Sun Temple, Puri
Biggest railway line	Dibrugarh to Kanyakumari
Biggest tributary river	Yamuna river
Biggest river in the south India	Godavari
Highest honor	Bharat Ratna
Highest bravery honor	Paramvir Chakra
Biggest Gurudwara	Golden Temple, Amritsar
Biggest church	Saint Cathedral, Goa
Highest T.V tower	Pitampura, New Delhi
Biggest beach	Marina beach, Chennai
Biggest artificial lake	Govind Sagar
Deepest river valley	Bhagirathi and Alaknanda
Biggest river island	Majuli, Brahmputra river (Assam)
Biggest planetarium	Birla planetarium
Highest air-strip	Lek, Laddakh
Biggest mansion	Rashtrapati Bhavan
Biggest road	Grand Trunk Road
Biggest gate	Buland Darwaza
Biggest river	Ganges
State with highest number of neighbors	Uttar Pradesh (8 neighbors)
Biggest newspaper factory	Nepanagar, M. P.

Mausoleums

Shanti Van	Jawaharlal Nehru
Mahaprayan Ghat	Dr. Rajendra Prasad
Kisan Ghat	Choudhary Charan Singh
Shakti Sthal	Indira Gandhi
Vir Bhumi	Rajiv Gandhi
Chaitya Bhumi	Bhimrao Ambedkar
Narayan Ghat	Gulzari Lal Nanda
Abhaya Ghat	Morarji Desai
Samta Sthal	Jagjivan Ram

United Nations Organization

- UNO was established on 24th October, 1945.
- Its main office is in New York and it has 193 member countries.
- The flag of the UNO has light blue background with the emblem of the UNO printed on it in white color. It has two curved olive branches with map of the world between them.
- English, French, Chinese, Arabic and Russian are the official languages of the UNO .

International Years Declared by the UNO

2012 International Year of Cooperatives

2013 International Year of Water Cooperation

2014 International Year of Solidarity with the Palestinian people.

2015 International Year of Light and Light-based Technologies

2016 International Year of Pulses

2017 International Year of Sustainable Tourism for Development

2019 International Year of Indigenous Languages

2022 International Year of Artisanal Fisheries and Aquaculture

2024 International Year of Camelids

International Decades Declared by UNO

2006-16 Decade of Recovery and Sustainable Development of the Affected Region

2018–2028 International Decade for Action "Water for Sustainable Development"

2019-2028 United Nations Decade of Family Farming

2021-2030 International Decade of Ocean Science for Sustainable Development

UN Special Agencies and Other Organizations

Agencies	Years	Headquaters
Intl. Telecommunication Union	**1865**	Geneva
Intl. Labor Organization	**1919**	Geneva
World Bank	**1945**	Washington DC
Food and Agriculture Organization	**1945**	Rome
Intl. Monetary Fund	**1945**	Washington DC
UNESCO	**1946**	Paris
Intl. Oceanic Organization	**1948**	London
World Health Organization	**1948**	Geneva
Intl. Finance Corporation	**1956**	Washington DC
World Intellectual Property Organization	**1967**	Geneva
United Nations Environment Fund	**1972**	Kenya
United Nations Population Fund	**1969**	New York
World Trade Organization	**1995**	Geneva

Other International Organizations

Agencies	Years	Headquarters
Commonwealth	**1931**	London
Arab League	**1945**	Cairo
Amnesty Intl.	**1961**	London
Red Cross	**1863**	Geneva
African Union	**1963**	Vienna, Austria
Group-77	**1964**	Geneva
Asian Development Bank	**1966**	Manila
Organization of South-East Asian Countries	**1967**	Jakarta, Indonesia
South Asian Regional Cooperation Organization	**1985**	Kathmandu, Nepal
Asia Pacific Economic Cooperation Organization	**1989**	Singapore
Group-15	**1989**	Geneva

Main Organs of the UN

General Assembly This is the only organ of the UN which offers membership to all its member countries with equal voting right. Its meeting is conveyed at least once every year. This meeting is generally held in September month in New York.

Security Council It is an instructive organ dealing with international peace and safety. It has five permanent members: USA, France, Britain, China and Russia. These countries will remain permanent members as long as the Security Council remains in existence. Each permanent member has Veto right. Even if one of the countries votes against a motion, that motion gets rejected. Security Council has 10 impermanent members also which are elected by the General Assembly for a term of two years. All the countries head the Security council for one month each, they are selected by alphabetical order.

Economic and Social Council This council has **54 members**. It deals with international affairs except those dealing with warfare and ammunition. It studies economic, social, and educational and health related issues and prepares its reports. It then sends its suggestion to General Assembly or other concerned organizations.

International Court It has 15 members, these are elected by General Assembly and Security Council. Only the people well-versed in international law can get appointed as judge at this court. Their tenure is 9 years and there is no restriction on their re-election.

Trust Council This council deals with the administration and security of the countries which did not gain independence after the second world war. It dealt with 11 countries out of which British Togoland, French Togoland, Cameron, Somaliland, Tanganyika, and Western Samoa have gained independence.

Secretariat This is the administrative organ of the UN. The Secretariat has a General-Secretary and other officers. The General-Secretary is appointed by the General Assembly on recommendation from the Security Council.

Internal Security System of India

Agencies	Year	H.Q.
Intelligence Bureau	1920	New Delhi
National cadet Corps	1948	-
Regional Army	1948	-
Central Reserve Police Force	1939	-
Central Bureau of Investigation	1953	-
Indo-Tibetan Border Police	1962	-
Home Guards	1962	-
Border Security Force	1965	-
Central Industrial Security Force	1969	-
Coast Guard Force	1978	-
National Security Guard	1984	-
National Crime Records Bureau	1986	-
Rapid Action Force	1992	-
Assam Rifles	1835	Shillong

Indian Classical Dances

Bharatanatyam	Tamilnadu
Kuchipudi	Andhra Pradesh
Odisi	Odisha
Manipuri	Manipur
Kathakali	Kerala
Attam	Kerala
Kathak	Uttar Pradesh and Rajasthan

International Weeks

1–7 February -World Interfaith Harmony Week

21–27 March-Week of Solidarity with the Peoples Struggling against Racism and Racial Discrimination

19–23 April - Global Soil Week

24–30 April-World Immunization Week [WHO]

8-14 May 2017-UN Global Road Safety Week [WHO]

25–31 May-Week of Solidarity with the Peoples of Non-Self-Governing Territories

World Breastfeeding Week [WHO]

4–10 October-World Space Week

24–30 October-Disarmament Week

6–12 November -International Week of Science and Peace

13–19 November-World Antibiotic Awareness Week,

Army Training Institutes of Indianh

Military

- National Defense Academy(NDA), Khadagwal (near Pune)
- National Defense College, New Delhi
- Indian Military Academy (IMA), Dehradun
- Indian Service Staff College, Wellington (Tamilnadu)
- Infantry School, Mau
- Armed Center, Ahmednagar (Maharashtra)
- Artillery School, Deolali

Navy

- I.N.S Chilka, Bhubaneshwar
- I.N.S Tisarcourse, Vishakhapatnam
- I.N.S Garud, Kochi
- I.N.S Shivaji, Lonowala
- Navy Academy, Goa

Air Force

- Air Force Administrative College, Coimbatore
- Air Force Academy, Hyderabad
- Air Force Technological College, Jalahali (Bengaluru)
- Paratrooper Training School, Agra

Folk Dances of India

Assam Bihu, Khel Gopal, Kali Gopal, Boi Saju

Punjab Nat Puja, Kikali, Bhagra, Gidda

H. P. Jadda, Nati, Chamba, Chhapeli

Haryana Dhamal, Khoria, Faag, Dahikal

Maharashtra Lejhijam, Tamasha, Lavni, Koli

J& K Damali, Hikat, Dandi Nach, Rau

Rajasthan Gangour, Jhoomar, Ghoomar, Jhoolan Lila

Gujrat Garba, Dandiya, Ras, Panihari, Ras Lila

Bihar Jat-Jatin, Ghumkadiya, Kirtaniya, Panwaria

U. P. Danka, Jhinka, Chhau, Lujhri, Jhora

Kerala Bhadrakali, Paydani, Kudiattam, Kaliattam

M. P. Diwali, Chait, Rina, Tapadi, Saila Hulko

W. Bengal Karankathi, Gambhira, Jalaya, Boul

Tamilnadu Kolltam, Karagam, Kavdi, Kummi

Arunachal Pradesh Mukhouta dance, Yuddh dance

Nagaland Kuminaga, Rengamnaga, Lim, Chong, Khaiva

Awards and Honors

National Awards

- **Bharat Ratna**: This is the highest honor of the country. This award was established in 1954. It is conferred for outstanding contribution in the field of arts, literature, science and other fields. The words Bharat Ratna are engrave on the shield, national emblem is printed on the backside with Satyamev Jayte is writtem under it.
- **Padma award**: This is the second highest award of the country. This too was established in 1954. It has three categories: Padma Vibhushan, Padma Bhushan and Padma Shree.

Bravery Awards

- **Paramvir Chakra**: This is the highest award conferred for bravery.
- **Mahavir Chakra** • **Vir Chakra**
- **Ashoka Chakra**: This is the peace-time bravery award.
- **Kirti Chakra** • **Shourya Chakra**

Literary Awards

- **Academy Awards**: Sahitya Academy award, Sangeet Natak Academy award, Lalit Kala Academy award.
- **Iqbal Award**: this award is given by Madhya Pradesh government for contribution in the Urdu literature.
- **Gyanpith Award**: this is India's most prestigious literary award. It is organized by Bhartiya Gyanpith Sanstha. It is a cultural organization established by Shanti Prasad Jain in 1949.

Science and Technology Awards

- **Shanti Svroop Bhatnagar Award**: this award is presented by Scientific and Technological Research Council of India.
- **Bhabha Award**: This award is presented for outstanding contribution in the field of atomic research. It is presented by Society of Nuclear Medicine.
- **Hariom Ashram Award**: This award is presented by U.G.C.
- **Borlaug Award**: This award is presented by Coromandel Fertilizers Limited every year.
- **Sarabhai Award**: This award is presented on 12th August every year on the birthday of Dr. Sarabhai.
- **Kalinga Award**: This award was started by Biju Patnayak, ex-Chief Minister of Odisha, for popularizing science.

Film and Music Awards

- **Dadasaheb Falke Award**: It is presented by Information and Broadcasting Ministry.
- **Tulsi Samman**: It is presented by the government of Madhya Pradesh for contribution in the field of tribal arts.
- **Kalidas Samman**: This award is presented by government of Madhya Pradesh for contribution in the field of theatre and performing arts.
- **Lata Mangeshkar Award**
- **National Film Award**

Other Awards

- **Bhartendu Harishchandra Award**: it was started by Information and Broadcasing Ministry in 1983.
- **Jamnalal Bajaj Award**
- **Dhanvantri Award**: This award is presented in the medical field.
- **Indira Gandhi Peace Prize**: It is presented for the contribution in the field of international peace, disarmament, communal equality and harmony.
- **Pt. Jawaharlal Nehru Award** for International Understanding

International Awards

- **Nobel Award**: It was established in 1901 in accordance with the will of Alfred Nobel, the inventor of dynamite. It is presented every year on 10 December.
- **Raman Magsaysay Award**: It was started in 1958 in the memory of Raman Magsaysay, the ex-president of Philippine. It is also known as the Nobel of Asia.

Literary Journalistic Awards

- **Pulitzer Award**: It was started by American publisher Joseph Pulitzer in 1971.
- **E. M. Forster Award**: It is presented to Indian writer for contribution in English literature.
- **The Booker Prize**: It is presented for the annually for the best novel.
- **Man Booker**: It is considered the highest prize in the field of literature after Nobel Prize.

Film Awards

- **Oscar Award**: This award is presented by National Academy of Motion Picture and Sciences since 1929.
- **Grammy award**

Sports

- **Olympics**: These games were started in 776 B.C. the modern Olympics were started in 1896 A. D in Athens, Greece. These are organized after every four years. India participated in the 1900 A. D Olympics for the first time.
- **Commonwealth Games**: These games were earlier known as British Empire Games. The first Commonwealth Games were organized in 1930 in Hamilton, Canada. These were first broadcasted on T.V in 1954(from Vancouver). These games were not organized in 1942 and 1946 due to the Second World War. These games are organized between two Olympic Games.
- **Asian Games**: The first Asian Games were organized in March, 1951 at New Delhi. Its emblem is shining sun.
- **SAARC Games**: These games were first organized in 1986 at Kathmandu, Nepal. These games were started to form cooperation and friendship among SAARC athletes.

Hockey

- It is the national game of India.
- The highest Astroturf (rubber field) of India is located at Silaru, H.P.
- **Perimeter**: length 91.44 meters and breadth 50-55 meters.
- **Related terms**: Right Back, Left Back, Outside Right, Center Forward, Center Half, Center Line, Corner Stroke, Tie Breaker, Sudden Death.
- **Important Trophies**: Hockey World Cup, Rangaswami Cup, Beighton Cup, Dhyanchand Trophy, Agha Khan Cup, Ajlan Shah Cup, Lal Bahadur Shashtri Cup, Maharaja Ranjit Singh Gold Cup

Badminton

- It is played on a court.
- **Perimeter**: Single Court is 44 feet long and 17 feet wide, the Double Court is 44 feet long and 20 feet wide.
- **Related terms**: Court, Shuttle, Racket, Side Line, Center Line, Net, Fault, Double Fault, Backhand Smash, Cross Shot, Late drop, Match Point.
- **Important Trophies**: Uber Cup, Rahmatullah Cup, Sudiraman Cup, Abdul Rahman Cup, Narang Cup, Mayor's Cup, China Cup.

Football

- The world's biggest football organization is International Football Association (FIFA).
- India's first football club was Dalhousie Club.
- **Perimeter**: football field is 91-120 meters long and 45-91 meter wide.
- **Related terms**: Center, Midfield, Strike, Back, Forward, Goalie, Kick, Free Kick, Direct Kick, Indirect Kick, Corner Kick, Off Side, Second Half, Handball, Tie Breaker, Sudden Death, Caesar's Kick.
- **Important Trophies**: FIFA Cup (World cup), Euro Cup, Copa-America Cup, European Champion Club Cup, Santosh Trophy, Durand Cup, Rover's Cup, Subroto Cup.
- **Famous Stadiums**: Webley (London, England), Salt Lake Stadium (Kolkata)
- Football originated in England. The first football club was formed in 1857, it was named Sheffield Football Club.

Tennis

- Tennis is a racket sport that can be played individually against a single opponent (singles) or between two teams of two players each (doubles).
- **Perimeter**: The perimeter of a standard tennis court used for playing doubles is 288 ft. The width of the court is 42 ft less than the length.
- **Related terms**: Back court, Service line, T or Middle T, Baseline, Center service line, Center mark, Service box, Side T, etc.
- **Important Trophies**: Davis Cup, Heineken Cup, French Open, Hopman Cup,Tata Open, U. Thant Cup, US Open,

Boxing

- **Perimeter**: The boxing ring is 4.9 4.9 to 6.10 6.10 M^2. It is fenced with three ropes on all four sides. The ring is 90 to 122 CM high from the ground.
- **Related terms**: Bounce, blow, belt, auxiliary, point, system, rapid punch, brake, cut, defense, down, hook, jab, knock out, round, upper cut, lower cut, second out, kidney punch.
- **Important Trophies**: Light Flyweight – up to 49 kg, Flyweight – up to 51 kg, Heavyweight - up to 91 kg, Super Heavyweight – above 91 kg.

Basketball

- This game was invented by James Smith in 1891.
- **Perimeter**: The court is 28 X 15 meter, the diameter of the ring is 45 cm, the length of the basket is 40 cm, the height of the basket from ground is 3.05 meter and the ball weight is 600-650 grams.
- **Related terms**: Foul out, guard, goal point, time watch, stop watch, center line, side line, dribble, double foul, center, front court, free throw, field goal, head goal, referee, timekeeper, scorer, jump wall, playing, time, ring, intermission, shifting zone, continuity pass, dead ball, basket hanging, personal contact, back board, lead pass, floating sideways.
- **Important Trophies**: America Cup, Muniswami Cup, William Todd Memorial Trophy, Prince Basalat Jha Trophy, Golden Eagle Trophy, European Championship, National Championship.

Volleyball

- This game was started by William G. Morgan (an American) in 1895 A.D.
- International Volleyball Federation was established in 1947 at Paris, it was transferred to Lausanne (Switzerland) in 1948.
- **Perimeter**: Volleyball court is 18 meter long is 9 meter wide. Net-height is 243 cm.
- **Related terms**: rotation, double hit, blocking, dig, net, net fault, service.
- **Important Trophies**: World Cup, Grand Champions Cup, Shivangi Gold Cup.

Polo

- Four players (mounted on horses) play in each team.
- **Perimeter**: Polo field is 275m long and 183m wide. Goalpost is 7.32m wide and 3.05m high.
- **Related terms**: Chucker, ball, goal, hook, bunker, mallet, galloping, free hit.
- **Important Trophies**: Ezra Cup, Prithvipal Singh Cup, Radha Mohan Cup, Classic Cup.

Kho-Kho

- **Perimeter**: Its court is 27m long and 15m wide.
- **Related terms**: Change, active, chaser, runner, cross-lane.

Billiards

- **Perimeter**: The table is 3.7m long, 1.85m wide and 3 feet high.
- **Jargon**: Cue, brake point, hazard.

Rifle Shooting

- **Related terms**: target, bull's eye, trench shooting, skeet shooting, muzzle etc.

Cricket

- The first Test Cricket match was played in 1877 and the first One day match was played in 1971 between Australia and England at Melbourne.
- **Perimeter**: The cricket pitch is 20.11m long. Stumps height is 28 inches.
- **Related terms**: over, stumped out, bowled, runner, spin, googly, boundary, Chinaman, flight, swing, full toss, short pitch, follow on, pitch, crease, umpire, innings, gloves, fielder, short run, over the wicket, cover, extra cover, mod on, mid-off, mid-wicket, slip, point.
- **Important Trophies**: World Cup, T-20 World Cup, I.C.C Trophy, Dilip Trophy, Ranji Trophy, Devdhar Trophy, Vijay Hazare Trophy, Irani Trophy, Ashes (Australia-England 5 test match series)
- **Important Stadiums**: Wankhede Stadium (Mumbai), Lords (London, England), Melbourne (Australia), Firozshah Kotla Stadium (Delhi), Eden Garden (Kolkata).

Golf

- The modern Golf originated in Scotland.
- The golf ball weighs 45.9 gram, its circumference is 4.27cm and the diameter of the hole is 4 inches.
- **Perimeter:** golf course is 5500-6000m (125-175 acres) long. It can be divided into maximum 18 holes.
- **Related terms:** best ball, dormy, fried egg, greed holes, links, putt, rough, tee, bunker, club, banana ball, double eagle, dough, bagel, mashie.
- **Important Trophies:** Circuit Cup, Backer Cup, Rider Cup, Dunhill Cup.

The Number of Players in Different Games	
Baseball	9
Rugby/Football	15
Polo	4
Water Polo/Netball/Kabaddi	7
Kho-Kho	9
Hockey/Football/Cricket	11
Volleyball	6
Tennis	1 or 2
Basketball	5
Gymnastics	8